MAKING A VIRTUE OF NECESSITY:
AN OVERVIEW OF THE ENGLISH
LANGUAGE IN NIGERIA

MAKING A VIRTUE OF NECESSITY:
AN OVERVIEW OF THE ENGLISH LANGUAGE IN NIGERIA

By

AYO BANJO
Professor of English Language
University of Ibadan
Ibadan, Nigeria

IBADAN UNIVERSITY PRESS
1996

Publishing House
Ibadan University Press
University of Ibadan
Ibadan, Nigeria

© Ayo Banjo 1996

First Published 1996

All Rights Reserved

ISBN 978 — 121 — 246 — 2

Printed by Johnmof Printers Limited Ibadan

Dedication

In Memoriam

Samuel Ayodele Banjo
1901 - 1980

CONTENTS

		Page
Preface		ix
1.	Determinants	1
2.	Nigerian Use of English	61
3.	Aspects of Nigerian Billingualism	95
4.	The Literary Use of English in Nigeria	121
5.	Prospects	149
Bibliography		157
Index		165

Preface

The English language has become the most important language in the world today, and its position has been compared with that of Latin in medieval times. Not surprisingly, therefore, the language has been discussed in a very large number of publications ranging from diachronic and synchronic grammars of the language to its sociolinguistics in different parts of the world.

A substantial number of persons around the world speak English as a second language, and the fate of the language in such situations has also been the object of study during the last quarter of a century. In West Africa, the pioneering publication in this connection was Spencer (1971) which presents a picture of the way in which the language had been adapting to its relatively new West African surroundings. Two years later, Sey (1973) examined those processes of adaptation in Ghana and broached the thorny problem of standards of correctness, a problem that had already begun to generate a lively debate in Nigeria. Sey's book on Ghana was followed six years later by Ubahakwe's (1979) in which the various functions and varieties of the English language in Nigeria were discussed by a galaxy of Nigerian linguists. Various aspects of the English language in Nigeria continued to be discussed in learned journals, as the present book points out, but three which have come out in book form deserve to be mentioned, namely, Kujore (1985) Jowitt, (1991) and Schmied (1991), the last presenting a panoramic view of the English language in the entire continent of Africa.

Following such previous work and given the importance that the study of the sociolinguistics of the English language in Nigeria has assumed in the Nigerian universities, as well as the growing debate over an optimal language policy for Nigeria, it is perhaps not too soon to have a study such as the present one which attempts, from the perspectives of an individual writer, to provide an overview of the language since its earliest contacts with what is now known as Nigeria. It is an attempt to see what wood emerges from the individual trees that have been described over the years and, hopefully, a challenge to other scholars to fill in the gaps which are obvious in the book. One such gap, and an important one, is the paucity of illustrative data even from the three main Nigerian languages, not to talk of the hundreds of other Nigerian languages. Such data are only just emerging in print, and it is hoped that the efforts will receive a fillip from a study such as this.

The phenomena described in this book are by no means peculiar to Nigeria. As Schmied (1991) has shown, they are replicated all over Anglophone Africa, and as Kachru(1966), Bailey and Gorlach(1982) and Pride (1982), among others, have further shown, they are shared with practically every country - particularly in South Asia - in which English is used as a second, rather than a foreign, language.

The English language made its debut in what is now known as Nigeria in the sixteenth century as a foreign language while at the same time producing a pidgin. In the middle of the nineteenth century, with Christian missionary activity in southern Nigeria during the period of informal colonization, the learning of the language became institutionalized. As the educational system expanded, social varieties of the language began to emerge, and Nigerian Pidgin, originally a medium of international communication, became primarily one of internal communication among the various peoples, particularly in the coastal areas.

At the beginning of the twentieth century, following formal colonization and the birth of Nigeria as one political entity, the language became the country's official language and the lingua franca among the educated classes. As more and more people had access to formal education, the social varieties of English became more and more pronounced. With national independence in 1960 came a growing concern about the position of English in the country and the desire for an endoglossic national language. And today, the debate is whether there should not, in addition, be an endonormative model of English to be cultivated in the country's educational system.

PREFACE

The pages that follow attempt to examine how through all the changes and chances, the English language has been affected by the linguistic environment and has, in turn, affected not only the linguistic habits of Nigerians but their very lives as well. Through the centuries of contact, certain elements have remained constant: the indigenous Nigerian languages, Nigerian Pidgin, and local varieties of English based on the length and quality of exposure to the language. Attitudes to each of these elements have changed from time to time, as has also the importance that each has assumed, but no optimal language policy is possible without due regard to each one of them and to the role that it should play in the twin processes of national integration and modernization.

The writing of this book was made possible through the generous extended sabbatical granted me by the University of Ibadan, for which I am very grateful. The writing began at the University of Cambridge, England, and was completed at Agder College, Kristiansand, Norway. I am deeply indebted to the authorities of these two institutions, particularly to the Director and staff of the Research Centre for English and Applied Linguistics at Cambridge, the staff of the English Department at Agder College, Kristiansand, Norway and the Norwegian Research Council for putting all necessary facilities at my disposal. The last supported my work in Kristiansand with a very generous grant. My indebtedness to colleagues is evident in the pages that follow, and I also wish to thank all of them. And finally, my deep and grateful thanks go to the members of my family for their constant support.

Ayo Banjo

1

The Determinants

In this chapter, we discuss a set of determinants which have guided and shaped the development of the English language through the centuries of contact between the language and the peoples of what is now known as Nigeria.

It is important to bear in mind that although Nigeria as a political entity only dates back to 1914 when Lord Lugard amalgamated the Northern and Southern Protectorates, the English language had, in fact, been taught institutionally in the area now known as Nigeria from about the middle of the nineteenth century, in such institutions as the Hope Waddell Institute, Calabar, the C.M.S. Grammar School, Lagos and St. Andrew's College, Oyo. Moreover, there are records attesting to the presence of the language in the same area since the eighteenth century, and in West Africa generally since the sixteenth century. Thus the English language was there before the political entity known as Nigeria was inaugurated. Nevertheless, for convenience, we shall speak as though Nigeria had been in existence in the seventeenth century but must be understood to be speaking of an identifiable area rather than a political entity (1).

A. Agencies:

1. *Commerce*

It is possible to identify the various agencies which have been responsible for the course that the implantation and development of the English language has taken in Nigeria. The earliest of these agencies is commerce. As a number of writers (e.g. Spencer, 1971) have noted, the English language was brought to Nigeria by English traders who had been active along the West African coast from as far back as the sixteenth century. Spencer (1971) quoting Hakluyt, notes that:

> William Hawkins the Elder made three voyages to Brazil between 1530 and 1532, each time calling at the Guinea Coast en route for the New World.

The first parts of the Guinea Coast to receive the linguistic as well as commercial impact of these visits were, ostensibly, territories west of Nigeria, and we do not as yet have a detailed account of the progress of European, and particularly English, commercial activity eastward to the coastal regions of Nigeria. However, we do know that by the eighteenth century, even before the ascendancy of the slave trade, English traders had established themselves in places like Bonny and Calabar. Certainly, by 1804, Archibald Dalzell, according to Hallett(1964) was able to declare that:

> at Bonney and Calabar there are many Negroes who speak English; and there is rarely a period that there are not at Liverpool, Callabar negroes sent there expressly to learn English.

We can only speculate about the earliest form of English that the English traders brought to Nigeria although, as we have just seen, by the end of the eighteenth century, Nigerians were already going to England to acquire the language. Indeed, the beneficiaries of these overseas courses lost no time, on their return to Nigeria, in establishing local schools for the propagation of the language.

There are two candidates for the earliest form of English to be spoken in Nigeria. One is Pidgin, and the other is a demotic form of English variously referred to as 'Broken English' or 'Minimal Pidgin', and it is necessary to make a distinction between the two, especially as both forms still survive side by side in Nigeria today. Indeed, there has been a tendency to subsume the two forms under the title of Pidgin.

Very useful work has been done in recent years on Nigerian Pidgin by such linguists as Mafeni (1971), Agheyisi (1971) and

Elugbe and Omamor (1991), and the verdict of all of them is that Pidgin is not a variety of English (i.e. not a dialect continuum of English) but a language in its own right. It is hardly necessary here to repeat the arguments leading up to this conclusion, but it has been demonstrated that although Nigerian Pidgin exhibits very marked English influence in its vocabulary, its grammar (i.e. its syntax and phonology) is much akin to that of the neighbouring indigenous languages.

The earliest contact of English with the indigenous Nigerian languages could not but have resulted in a pidgin, which is generally defined as a trade language precisely because of the circumstances in which it generally arises. Certainly the situation on the Nigerian coast accorded with the generally accepted ontogenesis of pidgin. The big question, however, is whether this pidgin developed *de novo* in Nigeria or had spread from other parts of the world (2).

To answer partially that last question, we can say with a degree of confidence that, in at least one sense, Nigerian Pidgin did not develop *de novo* from the contact with the English merchants. This is because there is evidence that a Portuguese-based Pidgin had predated the English-based variety on the Nigerian coast. Evidence of this is observable in the vocabulary of Nigerian Pidgin, and it is, of course, an undeniable fact that the Portuguese had preceded the English to the Nigerian coast. But this merely throws back the question to whether the Portuguese-based pidgin itself had developed *de novo* in Nigeria before a subsequent relexification.

There are, indeed, three schools of thought on this matter. One is that every pidgin starts from scratch in the unique circumstances in which it evolves. This view is held by such writers on the subject as Turner (1949) and Rens (1953). Later writers (e.g. Hancock, 1971) point out, on the other hand, that such a view would not allow a satisfactory explanation to be given for some of the features which creoles in various parts of the world do have in common. Hancock examines, in particular, lexical similarities between Sierra Leone Krio and Sranam, a creole spoken in Surinam, in north-eastern South America, and offers evidence to support the conclusion that both languages must have developed from a common pidgin. He then offers historical data to show that this original pidgin must have been taken to Surinam by slaves from West Africa in the middle of the seventeenth century when Surinam was under the English flag. However, it is not clear, going by the evidence offered, whether this original pidgin developed after the slaves arrived in Surinam, or whether, indeed, the slaves were already speaking the language before leaving West Africa. We must assume that either view is possible, given the fact, as previously indicated, that the English language had already made contact with the West African coast as far back as early sixteenth century, more than a century before the transportation of slaves from West Africa to Surinam.

We may next attempt to identify where roughly in West Africa this original pidgin had developed, and this should not be impossible to determine. The bulk of historical evidence points to territories west of Nigeria as the original theatre of activities of English traders, as of the Portuguese before them. If the original pidgin was imported from outside, therefore, it must have come from West African countries west of Nigeria.

It must be admitted, however, that the evidence is somewhat confusing. In the first place, Krio, the best-known creolisation of English in West Africa, shows a remarkable Nigerian - and specifically, Yoruba - influence. This evidence may tempt us, perhaps in defiance of the historical facts, to claim that Nigeria was indeed the original home of the pidgin which later went across the Atlantic. Alternatively, we may conjecture that the Nigerian influence on Krio was a later phenomenon following the repatriation and settlement of slaves from America.

The second school of thought is, indeed, one which argues a common ancestry for all pidgins and creoles. This is on the basis of a number of similarities among these languages. Hancock (1971), for example, provides a comparative word-list between English and seven English-based creoles, namely, Krio, Sranam, Saramaccan, Cameroon, Jamaica, Gullah and Guyana. The similarities in the list are obvious, but should not be pressed too far. The processes of pidginization are not infinite, and we must expect similarities when these processes are applied to the same basis even when the substrates are different. What makes the theory of common **origin** plausible is, in addition to the linguistic evidence, the **historical one** of movement of people around the critical areas.

The third school of thought is that which claims, not only that all pidgins and creoles have a common origin, but that that common origin is a Portuguese-based pidgin. Again, some linguistic evidence in support of this view has been offered, and Mafeni (1971) suggests that such words in Nigerian Pidgin as *'sabi,* (know), *pikin* (child), *dash* (gift, give a present), *palava* or *plaba* (quarrel) may have been borrowed into Nigerian Pidgin from that source (i.e. Portuguese).' Again, the linguistic is reinforced by the historical evidence. An English-based pidgin had, apparently everywhere, been preceded by a Portuguese-based pidgin, just as the English traders had been preceded by the Portuguese ones. This, at any rate, is true of Nigeria.

But the Portuguese influence on Nigerian Pidgin is compatible with both the *de novo* and common origin theories. If a Portuguese-based pidgin had flourished before the arrival of the British in Nigeria, we may suppose that that fact made it easier for an English-based pidgin to be created to replace it, presumably by a process of relexification. The Portuguese common origin view would argue that a Portuguese-based pidgin had been imported into Nigeria and that relexification had then followed.

Returning to Nigerian Pidgin, we can postulate that the language originated on Nigerian soil without completely denying the specific theory of a Portuguese common origin. This we can do by suggesting that, to begin with, a Portuguese-based pidgin had developed in the country as a result of trade contact with the Portuguese. Moreover, it is possible that some of the Portuguese traders and sailors had come with the experience of a Portuguese-based pidgin elsewhere. Later, when the English displaced the Portuguese, relexification followed.

The most important consideration for us here, however, relates, not to the origins but to the status of Nigerian Pidgin, though in passing we may remark that the uncertainties surrounding the origins of pidgins and creoles, which are less than five hundred years old, provide sobering thoughts for scholars, if there are still any, who are interested in unravelling the origins of the human language.

After five hundred years, the ontological problems of pidgins still persist. The difficulty, obviously, is that no definitive grammar of any pidgin or creole has been provided anywhere, though fragments are to be gleaned from Mafeni (1971), Agheyisi (1971) and

Elugbe and Omamor (1991). Discussions on pidgins and creoles tend to centre around the vocabulary, and dictionaries of Sierra Leone Krio (Fyle and Jones, 1980) and of Jamaican Creole (Cassidy and Le Page, 1967) have been published. Yet the status of these languages must be determined, not just by the vocabulary, largely provided by the basis (which is English), but more importantly by the grammar (which is not English).

Precisely because of the predominance of English-derived vocabulary, English-based pidgins are all too often classified as dialects of English occupying the extreme basilectal point in the dialect continuum. Even the names sometimes used such as Pidgin English and English Pidgin predispose the languages to such a classification. A detailed and convincing argument for the independent status of Nigerian Pidgin - note the name - (and, by extension, all pidgins) is contained in Elugbe and Omamor (op. cit.). Here, we shall merely draw attention to the fact that, while admitting that the processes of reduction and simplification are universal to all pidgins, the syntactic strategies and phonological processes observable in Nigerian Pidgin compel us to classify it, not as an Indo-European language, but with the indigenous languages of Nigeria, and specifically of southern Nigeria. The absence of inflection and of such a highly productive transformation in English as passivization would undoubtedly cast a serious doubt on the suggested status of the langauge as a dialect of English. Phonologically, the smaller inventory of vowels, the use of tone rather than stress and the near total absence of the grammatical deployment of intonation also point in the same direction.

An important theoretical question that arises has to do with the relative importance of lexis, on the one hand, and grammar, on the other, in determining the status of a language. Since it is clear that the vocabulary of any language is the least stable aspect of the language, it has to be conceded that the grammar is a more reliable indicator. Recent studies in language-mixing (e.g. Banjo, 1983) would seem to bear this out. It is, for example, possible to have a *bona fide* Yoruba sentence such as the following in which ninety per cent or more of the words are English:

    1.   O ti run round building yen three times
           He/she/it perf. run round building that three times.
           (He/she/it has run round that building three times).

All the lexical items in that Yoruba sentence are English, the only Yoruba items being grammatical ones, namely, the pronoun subject (o), the perfective aspect marker (ti) and the demonstrative pronoun (yen). But notice also that the word order "building yen" (that building) conforms to the syntactic rules, not of English, but of Yoruba. A monolingual speaker of English with a good ear may in fact be able to 'figure out' the meaning of the Yoruba sentence.

Yet we may not gloss over the sociological aspect of the matter. It is true that many monolingual speakers of English who would not take the Yoruba sentence given above to be an English sentence in spite of the heavy English borrowing may consider the following (from Mafeni,1971:110) as being perhaps minimally English:

2. di drayva dem de kom.
   The driver pl. cont. come.
   (The drivers are coming)

Here, unlike in [1], all the items derive from English, and the monolingual Englishman's difficulty in readily comprehending the sentence is more phonological than lexical/syntactic. There are, it is true, systematic phonemic substitutions and the replacement of stress with tone; but these are also markers of the English speech of many Nigerians. Nevertheless, there are two syntactic points of interest even in [2] namely, the use of *dem* (them) as plural marker (or, at other times, subject pronominalization in which the plurality is marked) and the use of a free aspect marker *de* instead of the English *be + ing*. But since *dem* is readily associated with *them* the syntax does not pose an insurmountable problem.

All that this proves, however, is that [2] is nearer English than [1], and not that either sentence is English; which brings us to the central point. To say that Nigerian Pidgin is not a dialect of English is not to deny that it is *related* in some ways to English which, after all, is its basis. But not every relationship has to be dialectal. Some speakers of Nigerian Pidgin themselves are under the impression that the language is a form of 'poor man's English', an undeserved stigma that the language is having a great deal of difficulty living down. Much is also sometimes made of the fact that it does seem possible for a monolingual speaker of English to carry on a conversation with a speaker of Nigerian Pidgin. No detailed study of mutual intelligibility between the two languages has been carried out, and even if it were to turn out that the degree of mutual intelligibility was appreciable in particular cases, it needs to be ascertained that what is thought to be Pidgin in such cases is not in fact 'minimal Pidgin', which is a mixture of Pidgin and English, which some Pidgin speakers are capable of when communicating with non- Pidgin speakers. Moreover, as sociolinguists have discovered, intelligibility tends to be sociologically coloured and has never been the sole determinant of dialect status, as witness the pairs of languages Danish and Norwegian, and Spanish and Portuguese.

Our conclusion therefore must be that Nigerian Pidgin is related to English but is not a dialect of it.

We must now turn our attention to demotic forms of English, with which Pidgin has often been confused. Clearly, not every contact of English with an indigenous Nigerian language results in a pidgin. Earlier, we suggested that some demotic form of English might be the alternative candidate for the original 'form of English' first spoken in Nigeria. It is, however, important to bear in mind that in the absence of primary data, all that can be done at present is to speculate about what might have happened centuries ago. The theory of pidgin origin (without necessarily granting that pidgin is a dialect of English) is based on the generally accepted view of the development of contact languages. It is important to bear in mind that in such situations, two *groups* of people face each other in a communication situation, and neither group has either the time or the inclination to learn the language of the other.

We may contrast this with another situation in which *individuals*, rather than groups, are involved. As soon as Englishmen began to take up residence in Nigeria (first, to pursue trade, next to propagate religion and finally to rule the country, the better to exploit its resources) the need was felt to take on Nigerian servants at home and Nigerian unskilled labour at work. We have no reason to believe that Nigerian Pidgin was immediately transplanted to these new situations, nor that new pidgins were developed. Rather, in these situations, the Nigerian individuals concerned attempted from the beginning to speak the Englishman's language in communicating with him. But such Nigerians' first attempts must have sounded very much like pidgin, and that not necessarily to unsophisticated ears. There is, after all, the same urgency to communicate as in the development of pidgin, resulting in similar attempts at reduction and simplification, and an attempt to make the vocabulary (which is English in both cases) virtually bear the whole brunt of communication. Those who were observant spotted the difference and referred to the individuals' efforts as 'broken English' or even 'minimal pidgin'. Both terms in fact refer to a demotic form of English.

To put it perhaps rather starkly, we may say that the demotic forms of a language originate from a conscious language-learning situation (3) whereas a pidgin does not. In the development of a pidgin, as we have remarked, neither *group* is attempting to learn the language of the other, and the predominance of English vocabulary can be quite easily explained by the fact that most of the objects that the two groups had to talk about were being introduced by the English traders. It is important to remember that the indigenous languages also made contributions to the vocabulary in the registers peculiar to them.

Given the fact that demotic forms originate from a conscious learning situation, we expect these forms to be less stable than pidgin, and so they are. A demotic form is nothing but the minimal form of an interlanguage. With continued exposure to the target language it becomes continually refined and may end up in what has been described elsewhere (Banjo, 1971) as Variety II English. This kind of approximation to English, on the other hand, does not define Nigerian Pidgin and has been observed only in situations of decreolization - suggesting that a pidgin has to be creolized first, before the base language starts exerting a pull on it because the speakers of such creoles (e.g. in Sierra Leone and the West Indies) are bilingual in Creole and English.

We may illustrate an early form of demotic English with a passage from the famous diary of Antera Duke as quoted by Forde (1956). It is the entry for 8 February, 1786:

> 3.'at 5 a.m. in aqua Bakassey Crik and with fine morning and I git for aqua Bakassey Crik in i clock time so I find Arshbong Duke and I go longsider his canoa to I tak Bottle Beer to Drink with him and wee have caqli first

for new Town and stay for landing come way so we go town in 3 clock time so we walk up to plaver house sam time to putt grandy Egbo in palaver house and play all night Combesboch go way with 639 slave & Trotter.'

To see the difference between this and Pidgin, we may compare it with a nineteenth century Pidgin passage quoted by Mafeni (1971:96):

4. 'Brudder George ... send warship look um what water bar ab got, dat good, me let um dat. Brudder send boat chopum slave, dat good. E no send warship cappen no peakeme, no lookee face. No,no; no me tell you, No; Suppose you come all you mont full palaver, give e reason, whye do it, me tell you, you peake lie, you peakeed-n lie. Suppose my fader, or my fader come up from ground and peake me why English man do dat, I no sabby tell why.'

There may be people who are prepared to argue that even [4] is slightly adulterated, but the difference between it and [3] is clear. Apart from the obvious differences of syntax and lexicon (and even pronunciation, to the extent that the spelling is any guide) there is the even more striking difference of rhetoric (notice, for example, the use of repetition in [4]).

Now, it is just possible that at the same time that Nigerian Pidgin was developing between *groups*, a demotic form of English was also developing between *individuals*, and the two forms may even have influenced each other, since the speakers are not likely to have been able to tell the difference. All things considered, however, the balance of probabilities would appear to be in favour of Pidgin as the earliest linguistic by-product of the contact between English and the Nigerian indigenous languages. The demotic forms of English are likely to have developed after the foreign traders had decided to settle down in the country. The other type of situation which produced demotic forms will be discussed later in the appropriate context.

2. Religion

If the English langauge was brought to Nigeria through the agency of commerce, the grafting of the language to the Nigerian sociolinguistic scene was supervised by the Christian religion through missionary activity. As we do know that this activity dates back to 1842, when missionary efforts began in Badagry and at Abeokuta, the question arises, in passing, as to the status of the English language in Nigeria during the preceding two or three centuries.

If, as argued in the preceding section, the learning of the English language came in the wake of the development of Nigerian Pidgin, it follows that during the period preceding the nineteenth century, Nigerian Pidgin and English existed side by side. We have already seen evidence of this in the reference to Nigerians from Calabar area going to Britain in the eighteenth century to receive instruction in the English language, such Nigerians returning home to establish English language schools of their own; and to Antera Duke's Diary. So, attempts to learn the 'metropolitan' variety of English by no means originated from the nineteenth century. Rather, for a century or more before that, varieties of English had developed ranging from the demotic to the standard. If the diary of Antera Duke represents the former, the writings of Olaudah Equiano, Ottobah Cugoano and Ignatius Sancho typify various approximations to the latter.

But there is a difference not to be overlooked. Whereas Antera Duke learnt his English at home through a series of approximative systems as earlier postulated, Equiano, Cugoano and Sancho all had lived most of their adult lives in Britain. Equiano, for example, as noted elsewhere (Banjo,1970b) 'had been sold into slavery at the age of ten, and for the next eleven years had worked aboard slave ships sailing between the Caribbean and England. He had bought his freedom at the age of twenty-one, continued as a sailor for a few more years and ended up as the *Commisary of Stores* for the freed slaves returning to Sierra Leone.'

The slave trade, which raged in the eighteenth century with catastrophic consequences for West Africa, indeed added a new dimension to the story of the English language in West Africa by first linking up home-grown varieties of the language with the metropolitan variety brought back by manumitted slaves, and dispossessing many a West African of his indigenous language.

Nevertheless, English was still at this time a foreign language in Nigeria, confined to those who were active, first in the trade in goods, then in the trade in human beings, with the British, and the number of such English-speaking Nigerians must have been minuscule.

It was in the wake of the abolition of the slave trade that the missionaries came to Nigeria. Two conflicting explanations have been offered for their coming. One is that the Church in Britain was moved by the horrors of the slave trade and the reports of 'heathenism' in the area. By this explanation, the missionaries had therefore come to offer solace to the people and to open up their territories to Christianity. The other explanation is that they had come as the forerunners of imperialism to offer an anaesthetic to the people while the groundwork for the exploitation of their material and human resources was being laid. Certainly there is enough evidence to support either theory, and possibly both motives were present in the minds of at least some of the earliest missionaries. If the missionaries did not go out of their way to give active support for the exploitations going on all around them, they are not on record, either, as having raised a voice against them. The era of liberation theology was, as yet, more than a century, and thousands of miles, away.

Either explanation has important implications for the course of the English language in Nigeria from the nineteenth century. Whichever explanation we choose does not alter the fact that the missionaries, from the beginning, saw the necessity to train Nigerian auxiliaries for the work of evangelization. Here then was a new kind of encounter, different in form and texture from the one centuries before between Nigerians and the English traders at the ports. If the latter came with an eye to quick bargains and minimal contact, the former had come to change a people's way of life.

If we choose what we might refer to as the 'charitable' hypothesis - i.e. that the missionaries had nothing but humanitarian motives - then it is clear that the intention was to teach a 'superior' way of life and banish all ignorance and superstition. The vehicle of that crusade, naturally, was the English language, and we should not be surprised then if this language began to loom large in the lives of the missionaries' hosts. If, on the other hand, we choose the 'sceptical' hypothesis, the symbolism of the English language becomes even more intimidating. In either case, the dominance of the English language was assured from the very beginning.

The missionaries worked from the outset with repatriates from Sierra Leone, where large numbers of manumitted slaves had been settled from 1787. English education had naturally had a head start in Sierra Leone, from where a steady stream of repatriates moved eastward to Ghana and Nigeria, many of them in search of their roots, but all of them taking up the first white-collar jobs, first with the missionaries, and later in the civil service at the advent of colonialism. Perhaps the most famous of the repatriates was Samuel Ajayi Crowther, who later became the first African bishop and who served his native Nigeria for the rest of his life and was buried in his home town of Osoogun. Like Equiano, Crowther had been captured as a small boy and taken abroad as a slave.

Crowther's autobiography provides an instructive study in the once-popular and over-exploited theory of culture conflict.

While he accepted without questioning the rationale for the evangelization of his people and even the inferiority of his own race, he was also fired by genuine patriotism which led him to work relentlessly for the development of his mother tongue as well as of other indigenous Nigerian languages. He certainly was not one to feel that these languages were too tainted to be handled nor did he work for their replacement by the English language.

Crowther in a way represented the *via media* in the attitudes exhibited by Sierra Leonean repatriates in Nigeria in the nineteenth and early twentieth centuries. The majority attitude was, indeed, an assimilationist one. This arose from a wholesale acceptance of European racial superiority and had been fuelled by the cultural alienation that the years of slavery had brought about. Nor should the economic advantage of being assimilated be overlooked. Indeed, these repatriates provided a role model for the rising Nigerian elite who gradually absorbed and replaced them until they, in turn, were subsequently caught up in the nationalist movement. A typical exponent of the assimilationist view was Alex Crumwell, who roundly condemned African culture in his book (Crumwell, 1864). These Africans looked down on African languages and cultures, were embarrassed by them and even showed signs of being more Catholic than the Pope.

At the same time, there were those, like Edward Blyden, who were the earliest flagbearers for African nationalism. Such individuals were anxious not only to find their roots in Nigeria and elsewhere in West Africa but to be fully restored to them. Some of them changed their English names back to Nigerian ones and set the fashion for adopting Nigerian forms of dress. They were no less prominent personalities than the assimilationists - many of them, in fact, being Nigeria's earliest lawyers, doctors and engineers - but they rejected the theory of racial superiority and sought to inspire confidence in their compatriots.

One of the *lacunae* in the cultural history of Nigeria which it would be interesting to be able to fill is the exact nature of the communication between the earliest missionaries and the chiefs of Badagry and Abeokuta. Who were the interpreters? Some of the Sierra Leonean repatriates, perhaps, who had not completely lost their indigenous languages (some such individuals must also have helped earlier in Sierra Leone in the compilation of the *Polyglotta Africana*); or some Nigerians with a mercantile background who had the mastery of (minimal) Pidgin or of a variety of English? Such individuals played the historic role not only of linking the missionaries with their prospective proselytes, but perhaps more importantly, of linking one chapter of the development of the English language in Nigeria to the next, not to mention their agency in helping to bring about a comprehensive and fundamental transformation of their country.

However, whatever may be the answer to that conundrum, the missionaries settled down immediately to the urgent task of producing their own interpreters. Henceforth, the English language in Nigeria was no longer to be just at the service of commerce; it was now to bring about a new kind of elite. The learning of the language was no longer to be perfunctory; it was now to be institutionalized and, to all intents and purposes, perpetuated.

3. *Education*

There is no evidence to show that English as a foreign language in Nigeria had any impact on the indigenous systems of education between the sixteenth and the nineteenth centuries. It is true, as already noted, that 'schools' for producing interpreters had been established in the Calabar area as early as the eighteenth century. But these must have been *ad hoc* classes designed to impart the oral and probably also the literacy skills of English to would-be interpreters and clerks, rather than being integrated into the indigenous system. Such attempts to learn the English language must have been regarded esoteric, the majority of those having dealings with European traders being content to operate in one variety or another of Pidgin. Nor could it have crossed the minds of the European traders themselves to implant the English language in Nigeria in any systematic manner.

The missionaries, on the other hand, had come to stay, and had to solve the problem of communication between them and their hosts. Indeed, communication was the whole point of their business in the country, and not just minimal communication at that. It was, also, hardly to be communication between equals; on the contrary, the goal was some sort of cultural assimilation in which a new educational system was to provide an underpinning for the new religion. And so a new system of education came to be superimposed on the indigenous systems, the latter being banished more and more to the periphery until reduced to virtual non-existence.

Every church built by the missionaries had a primary school attached to it. Here pupils spent up to ten years and left with a primary school certificate which provided the holders with access to jobs not only in churches and schools but also in commerce and, later, the public service. One of the most important subjects on the curriculum was, naturally, English, and it must be said that the standards achieved in the language by the early products of the system became the great envy of their late twentieth-century progeny. Later, the missionaries went on to build secondary schools, and it is hardly surprising to find that the first one, as far as we know, was located in Calabar - the Hope Waddell Institute - where the Scottish Presbyterian Church had quickly established itself. But much of the missionary activity, in which the Anglican and Methodist Churches participated, was concentrated in the south-western parts of the country, with the Roman Catholic Church coming in later to establish in the south-eastern parts. The Baptists and other American denominations were later to penetrate the northern parts, though only with limited success.

For more than a century, the missionary societies held sway over the new Nigerian formal educational system in areas under their influence. They established the complete apparatus, including a very effective inspectorate machinery. Their system was so successful that the products of their secondary schools were able to receive university education in Britain itself without any apparent special difficulty, linguistic or otherwise.

With the inauguration of Nigeria as a single political entity, early in the twentieth century, the new government naturally took an interest in education but seemed unwilling either to replace or even compete with the missionaries. As a result, when colonial government finally came to an end on 1 October, 1960, the overwhelming majority of schools - particularly primary schools - were still under the control of voluntary agencies made up largely of Christian and Moslem bodies.

It has often been wondered whether the colonial government ever had a clear and unambiguous language policy for the colony, and whether they tried to influence the missionary schools in the light of such a policy. But first we may ask, what was the language policy of the missionary societies? Here the answer would appear to be, in a general kind of way, bilingualism in English and the mother tongue, with English dominance. At the same time, they saw to it that English became the language of instruction not later than the third year of a six and sometimes eight-year primary education programme, and brought to bear their earlier experience in other colonies such as India on the situation. On the other hand, they did encourage the teaching of the indigenous languages and supervised the publication of text-books in these languages. Thanks to leaders like Ajayi Crowther, the Bible was being translated into the indigenous languages and therefore it was necessary to promote literacy in these languages. The missionaries realized that they would be able to communicate most effectively with the masses and win their souls if they employed the indigenous languages.

The colonial government would appear to have had no strong views on the matter and was content to support the policy of the missionaries. To consolidate the dominance of English, it offered incentives for the teaching of the language, but at the same time gave support to efforts to provide text-books in the indigenous languages.

Together, the government and the missionaries ensured that the School Certificate, issued by the University of Cambridge, was equal in standard in every subject to any other issued by any other examining body in Britain or elsewhere.

But of course the colonial government had its own preoccupations which were by no means the same as those of the missionaries. They were administering the country as part of the vast British Empire on which the sun at that time never set, and the official language of the Empire was English. Like the missionary bodies, the government too needed local personnel to fill the middle and lower rungs of the civil service; but unlike the missionaries, they were not troubled about the souls of the indigenous population - and not too troubled about their bodies either, considering the wage structure. Law and order here and now was the chief concern of the government rather than a state of bliss in the hereafter. *Pax Britannica* had to be maintained and the colony must make its contributions to the empire. To this end the education of the elite was pursued and a few of them even filtered through to the top echelons of the public service. But the irony is that the English language which helped the colonial administrators to attain a high degree of efficiency in exploiting the colony also helped in the end to ensure the liquidation of the colonial government, for colonialism was fought on its own terms and in its own language.

The colonial government never expressly declared English as the official language of Nigeria. The tradition going back to the Roman Empire was simply assumed, namely, that the colonized adopt the language of the colonizer since the colonizer cannot be expected to operate in anything but his own mother tongue. Besides, ability to speak the language of the colonizer competently confers rich rewards. So there was no need to make a law, no need to compel Nigerians to learn the English language. But if not *de jure* the English language certainly became, *de facto* the official language of Nigeria. We shall examine the full implication of this at a later stage, but may here draw attention to one far-reaching consequence of this lack of an explicit policy on the English language.

This lack of an explicit policy is actually of one piece with the different political policies adopted to the northern and southern parts of the country. While the missionaries were active in the south, indirect rule was the declared policy in the north. The result of this is that in the second half of the twentieth century, the bulk of English-speaking Nigerian bilinguals were produced in the south, and Arabic was virtually as important in the north as English was in the south. This has encouraged the feeling that the country is made up of two distinct parts - North and South - resulting in seemingly intractable difficulties for the process of nation-building.

Since independence, the governments of the federation have exerted increasing influence on education, and their first impulse was to 'downgrade' the English language within the educational system as part of the new self-assertion. It is understandable that some of the Nigerian nationalists should look upon the English language as the symbol of colonialism. To such nationalists, the indigenous cultures could not possibly come back into their own unless the English language, together with its cultural baggage, was, if not totally eliminated, at least considerably reduced in importance in the national scheme of things. The campaign against the English language in Nigerian education - and, by implication, in Nigerian life - reached a climax in the early nineteen-sixties when a very vocal lobby succeeded in persuading the government to prevail on the West African Examinations Council not to make the award of the school certificate conditional on a pass in the English language paper. There were other Nigerians who counselled caution, pointing out the load that the language carried both within and outside the educational system. The facile theory of the alienating influence of English in Nigeria won the day, reinforced by the alarming evidence of plunging levels of performance in the subject in the examinations, and the change of policy was effected. It should be added, however, that in spite of the new policy, the universities continued to demand a pass at Credit level as a condition for admission to any of their Departments, though occasionally the condition was waived in favour of candidates presenting very good grades in the science subjects.

Nevertheless, within twenty years, there was a nation-wide outcry over falling standards, not only in English but in education generally, and there were those who saw a causal connection between the fall in English standards and that in education generally. Many Nigerians looked back with nostalgia on the inimitable performance in English of their fathers and grandfathers who had only possessed the Primary Six Leaving Certificate.

It must be granted that this feeling of falling standards in English competence is more impressionistic than scientifically validated, but some clear bases for the impression can be suggested. The change in attitude to the language, and to the teaching of it, is certainly one of them. Because a pass in the language no longer affects the profiles of school results, almost anybody is allowed to teach the language, particularly at the critical stages. But another explanation must certainly be found in the population explosion in schools which came in the wake of national independence. However, a study (Banjo, 1974) showed that the impression of falling standards was not borne out by School Certificate results, in which the percentage of passes at credit level had remained constant indicating, perhaps, that even the standards of marking, and possibly of the proficiency of the examiners themselves, were falling. Certainly, many factors were at work.

Rescue operation has taken various forms, and this is a subject to which we shall be turning our attention later. We may at this point simply note that the general attitude to the English language in Nigeria has undergone a number of changes since it became the undeclared official language of the country in the mid-nineteenth century. The first attitude, as we have noticed, was *assimilationist* at a time when the Sierra Leone repatriates dictated the fashion, and in the eyes of the rising Nigerian bilingual elite, there was power, influence and comparative affluence in possessing a good command of the English language. However, with the surge of nationalism, fuelled by the Indian independence in 1947, and the ideas of a steady stream of Nigerians returning home after studies in the United States of America, the attitude soon changed to a *nationalistic* one which questioned the language as much as it did the form of government itself. Some of the consequences of this attitude are as just noted above.

After a decade or so of independence, realism and a greater sense of proportions returned to the consideration of the position of the language in the country, and thus a *universalist* attitude has been ushered in. This is an attitude which encourages an instrumental motivation for learning the language and excelling in it; an attitude which recognizes English as the most important international language spoken in practically every corner of the world as mother tongue, a second language or a foreign language. This attitude has encouraged the adaptation and appropriation of the language for the country's practical and aesthetic needs, resulting in a crop of universally acclaimed Nigerian writers of English expression, one of them attaining the distinction of a Nobel Laureate.

That being the case, the country could now turn its attention to the important task of fashioning out a policy of language in education and in at least one important area of national life.

B. Policies:

This brings us to a consideration of policies with regard to the development of the English language in Nigeria. A national policy can only be as old as the nation, and so in the present case we do not expect any policies to have emerged before the beginning of the twentieth century. It is arguable, though, that the various missionary societies had policies relating to the schools of which they were proprietors. This is not the place to examine the larger issue of the missionary societies' educational policies and to ask what kind of individuals they aimed at producing. The policies can be described in the broadest terms as being to provide a christian education. The immediate beneficiaries of those policies would be the church itself. As we have noted, the missionaries aimed at producing bilinguals with English dominance. This was important because priests had to be trained - some of them being sent to England to finish off their training - and graduates had to be produced not only as preliminary training for priesthood, but also to run the secondary grammar schools and teacher training colleges. With the establishment of Fourah Bay College in 1827, a steady stream of Nigerians, sponsored in particular by the Church Missionary Society, sailed westwards to Freetown to receive undergraduate training and later to take up important positions in church, in education and, eventually, in State.

A good grounding in English was thus necessary for the kind of education aimed at. At a time when there was no university in Nigeria, the possibility had to be kept in mind of some at least of the products of missionary education studying side by side later with native speakers of English or the elite of Sierra Leone who were already very proficient in the language.

The colonial administrators, as already observed, were in some difficulty with regard to an English language policy in the country since conditions were kept different between the North and the South. Because the conditions were favourable, Hausa was promoted as a *lingua franca* in the North, and at the same time, the Islamic schools were allowed to continue to flourish. In the South, the government acquiesced in the proselytization of the population by the Christian missionaries and actively supported the teaching of English.

It could perhaps be argued that the difference in policy between the North and the South was inevitable. Not only had most of the North been islamized as a result, early in the nineteenth century, of the jihad spearheaded by Uthman dan Fodio, the Hausa language had also spread considerably in the region and had readily been adopted as a second language by those who did not speak it as their mother tongue. Over and above this, there was, politically, also an emirate system of government which had already taken root before the advent of the colonial administrators and which the new rulers were not inclined to disturb. There was, in contrast, no such cohesion in the South. The missionaries were attempting to provide a common religion, though in different denominations, but there was no overarching political system and no linguistic rallying force. Rather, the terrain varied politically between the Western Region which had evolved a sophisticated monarchical system and the Eastern Region which was republican in temperament. The hope, perhaps, was that the English language would provide a rallying force in the southern regions; but still, it was a great deal easier to define a Northerner than a Southerner, and neither the English language nor the Christian religion has been able to effect a meaningful meeting of minds among the disparate peoples of southern Nigeria.

It is thus hardly surprising that the first English-speaking bilinguals emerged from the south of the country, and this inevitably meant an early domination of the public service and of international commerce with Europe by individuals from this part of the country. The seeds of two nations in one had been sown, and it is difficult to fathom what long-term plans the colonial administrators could have had. One theory is that they really intended to administer the country as if it were two. Another is that they set out to create a country which would be perpetually at war with itself. Whichever theory is the truth or nearer the truth, the fact is incontestable that the colonial administrators took no early steps to produce a unified country but rather pursued policies which eventually led to an attempted Balkanization of the country.

But if more people in the south were learning the English language than in the north, it became clear by the second half of the twentieth century that the quality of English being spoken in the north was 'superior' to what could be heard in the south. By 'superior' is usually meant 'nearer Standard British English or Received Pronunciation.' This impression was so widespread in the first two decades of the second half of the twentieth century that it would be futile trying to deny it. Rather, we should seek an explanation.

We can look in two main directions for an explanation - first, the Hausa language itself, and secondly, the manner in which the English language was taught and used in the north. A contrastive study of English and twelve Nigerian languages (Dunstan, 1969) indeed shows that, at the phonemic level, Hausa has more in common with English than, say, Igbo or Yoruba, the other two dominant languages of Nigeria, both of them based in the south(5). At the suprasegmental level, Hausa also makes use of both the features of tone and stress, whereas Yoruba and Igbo each only has tone. The result is that the Hausa speaker is better predisposed to produce the English isochronicity of stress. However, in syllable structure, Hausa is not much different from the other two major languages, and a Hausa speaker of English seems even to have a greater tendency to simplify English consonant clusters by supplying an intruding enclitic - e.g. /suku:l/ for /sku:l/ (school). In syntax, Hausa, unlike Yoruba or Igbo, also has gender, but does not share any more grammatical transformations with English than the other two languages. In the area of vocabulary, Hausa has no particular advantage either.

Thus it is largely in the area of pronunciation that the Hausa speaker of English is at an advantage over the speakers of the other two major Nigerian languages. It is true that this, in fact, is the aspect most readily observed, but the English of the Hausa speakers of the generation being considered was also thought to be somewhat more idiomatic than that of the southern speakers, and here we must seek an explanation both in the mode of teaching the language in the north and in the sociolinguistic position of English in the area.

Because British-type schools were few and far between in the north in the first half of the twentieth century, it was possible to run them properly, or at least more efficiently than in the south. At a time that pupils in the south had ceased to have direct exposure to native speakers of English, the language continued to be taught to pupils in the north by native speakers. Thus exposure to native-speaker models further enhanced the predisposition of the pupils to learn the language, and much smaller enrolments in schools than in the south further meant that teachers were better able to give individual attention to the pupils. It is hardly surprising, therefore, that there was a higher proficiency in spoken English in the north than in the south.

But perhaps even more important was the fact that in the early days of colonial administration, the English language in the north was virtually a foreign language whilst in the south it was rapidly developing into a second language. The fact already noted was responsible for this, namely, that whereas there was a need to use English as a lingua franca across the south, there was no such need for the language in the north, where Hausa had already established itself in the secular domains and Arabic in the religious ones. As a result, fewer registers of English were needed in the north than in the south, and it was possible to learn the fewer registers more efficiently than perhaps would have been possible had a wider range of the language been attempted.

It is customary to recognize up to five tenors in the English language to suit the communication situation. These are *frozen, formal, consultative, informal,* and *intimate.* The native speaker of the language is able instinctively to choose the appropriate tenor to suit a speech event whereas, as copiously noted by previous writers on the subject, speakers of English as a second language have problems in this area which they may never be able to overcome completely. Speakers of English as a *foreign* language, however, do not have quite the same problem since the communication situations are likely to be highly restricted. They are, in fact, likely to be restricted to the more formal situations. The picture that emerges in Nigeria in the early decades of colonization was, indeed, one in which while the English langauge was restricted to formal occasions in the north, it was already being made to serve both formal and informal situations in the south. Inevitably, the language started taking on local 'colour' - as a result of widespread mother tongue transfers - in the south at a much faster rate than in the north. The observation by Kirk-Greene (1971:128) is apposite:

> '...in the classical emirates of Northern Nigeria, the strong preference for the use of Hausa as the language of wider communication outside school has relegated English to the status of a classroom language. By comparison, in the southern areas of Nigeria, where the Kwa languages are dominant, the lack of an alternative lingua franca means that English is very much the daily language of schoolchildren both outside and inside the school.'

The phenomenon is a universal one, that competent speakers of a language as a foreign language tend to sound more like the native speakers of the language than second-language speakers of the language are likely to do. Their needs are considerably less, and so they are able to satisfy them more successfully. At the same time, the native model exerts a much stronger influence on a foreign-language speaker than on a second-language one. Indeed, in the generality of cases, the foreign- language speaker learns the language in order to be able to communicate with the native speakers. The second-language speaker, on the other hand, by definition, learns the language in order to be able to communicate more with other second-language speakers than with the native speakers, and soon begins to look within his own society for standards of correctness.

With the advent of national independence, however, the whole picture underwent a rapid change. The inequities created by the different patterns of learning English in the north and south became all too glaring at independence in October 1960, and the Northern leaders decided to do something about them. A two-pronged attack was decided upon. On the one hand, British-type schools were rapidly established to augment the few elite ones already in existence. This inevitably liberated the same sociolinguistic forces that had been noticeable in the south for more than half a century. It meant, for one thing, that, as in the south, fewer and fewer pupils in the north were becoming exposed in the classroom to native-speaker models. Indeed, because many teachers were recruited from the south, it meant that southern models were spreading to the north while at the same time transfers from Hausa became increasingly noticeable (6). The age of 'the golden voices of the North' was rapidly disappearing. But not quite, because the second approach to the problem was to send many boys from the North to study in Britain at the secondary and tertiary levels to facilitate the catching up with the South. The recipients of these awards returned to continue the tradition of careful elocution in English, but it must be admitted that they had now been swamped by the home-grown bilinguals.

For almost a decade before the attainment of independence in 1960, the country was administered as three Regions - East, West and North. There was understandably keen rivalry between the Regions, and all of them recognized that education held the key to rapid development. But ironically, the proliferation of schools was accompanied by a fall in standards, and English, being a key subject, suffered more than any other subject. What policies towards English did the Regional governments pursue in the face of this deterioration?

Fresh from winning the battle against colonialism, the new leaders were by no means about to enthrone the language of the erstwhile colonizers. Yet the only option open to the country was an English-medium education. How were they to promote a rapid expansion in education while at the same time denigrating the medium of instruction within the system? The leaders tried to have their cake and eat it too. If poor performance in English was bringing about poor results in the School Certificate examination, then the importance of English in the examination had to be reduced. Many would consider what resulted as merely an illusion of progress. In any case, as already indicated, the universities knew better.

Yet the difficulty confronting the leaders should not be underestimated. Political independence was won as a result of a popular movement, and a better deal had been promised to everybody: the ranks of the elite were about to be swelled (much later, the same elite was to be blamed for all the ills befalling the country). So, education had to be expanded, if necessary beyond breaking point. The old established elite schools managed only for a short while to distance themselves from what was going on, until a ferocious policy of proletarianism in the following decade effectively took care of them, turning them into mere shadows of their former selves. What was required was levelling up: what was effected was levelling down. It is hardly surprising that in the circumstances the elite took to sending their children to Britain for secondary education, thereby attempting to perpetuate an English-speaking aristocracy.

One alternative that the leaders might have considered was a more gradual expansion of the system, but such a course would have been suicidal for the politicians with an eye on the next election. The other alternative was to follow a middle course in which, while fairly rapidly expanding the system, they strengthened the existing quality schools and made them serve as models. Such a course would indeed appear to have been resorted to, belatedly and curiously, with the establishment of Unity Schools whose educational function, as distinct from the political one, was to serve as pace-setters.

In less than twenty years after independence, another momentous change had also taken place: the religious bodies had been dispossessed of their schools. The work of the missionary societies was done, after a little less than one-and-a-half centuries, their institutions barely recognizable. Meanwhile, to emphasize the end of an era, voices had started to be raised in the call for a lingua franca or a national language which would take over from the English language.

At last, the need for a coherent language policy in education was being faced. This development was to be expected, but the problem was truly daunting. Here was a country with about four hundred languages, on which the English language had been superimposed as the official language. In the first half of the twentieth century, a pattern had, to be sure, been emerging in which three languages - Hausa, Igbo and Yoruba - had dominated the political landscape. This domination had been more effective in the North, as we have seen, but had not gone unresisted in the West or East. In the West, political restiveness quickly led in 1963 to the carving out of Mid-

West Region. But while this reduced the political influence of the former Western Region, it effectively turned it into a linguistically homogeneous State.

By the same token, the newly-created Mid-West Region became the most linguistically heterogeneous State in the country, and in this and other ways became a microcosm of the country itself. Because of the linguistic complexion of the Region, Nigerian Pidgin slowly but surely asserted itself as the lingua franca, creolising rapidly, in fact, in parts of the Region, particularly the Delta area.

The Eastern Region in the meantime remained politically intact but had never been linguistically homogeneous. While it is true that, before independence, Igbo had gradually been adopted as a second language outside its heartland, there was simmering political discontent in what were later to become Cross River and Rivers States, each of these States later, in turn, experiencing unrest of an ethnic/linguistic nature.

Next to the new Western Region, the Northern Region enjoyed the highest degree of linguistic harmony. But the Northern Region had never been linguistically homogeneous. It was just that conditions had been created there which favoured the spread of Hausa as a second language. Even in the Yoruba-speaking enclave of what later became Kwara State, loyalty to Hausa was for some time almost as strong as to Yoruba. Indeed, the Yoruba of the old North were a well favoured lot enjoying, as it were, the best of both worlds. Like the rest of Yorubaland, they were early beneficiaries of missionary education and produced a disproportionately high number of English-speaking Northerners. As a result, it meant that they represented an influential group in the Public Service of the North.

How did attitudes to English fit into the changing political scenes? Within a space of one decade (1960-1970) the political map of Nigeria had been redrawn twice. At independence, there were three Regions. Three years later, the number went up to four, and another four years later, the four Regions had been replaced by twelve States. The number of States in 1976 stood at nineteen, in 1987, twenty-one, and in 1991, thirty. The country was in search of an abiding basis for unity, and it cannot be denied that one of the most potent centrifugal forces was the multiplicity of nationalities and languages. Obviously, English, the official language, had failed to hold the diverse peoples of Nigeria together, and its failure was not any less spectacular in the South than between the South and the North. Education was on the concurrent legislative list, which meant that every Region - and later, every State - could decide its own educational policy.

The English language had now arrived at a peculiar position in the country. While it remained the country's official language, its status as a second language in the country was now being seriously undermined. Outside strictly official business, the language was no longer indispensable for internal communication in the States of the north, nor in the Western State, nor, indeed, in the two Igbo-speaking States of the former Eastern Region. In none of these States was the English language required to hold the people together; each of them could quite easily have proclaimed a lingua franca for itself. Ironically, the languages in these linguistically self-sufficient States were Hausa, Yoruba and Igbo, thus reasserting the prominence of the old 'three main languages of Nigeria.' Elsewhere in the south, Pidgin was effectively the lingua franca.

This provided a congenial climate in which to consider the future of the English language in the country, and the questions raised included the following:

(a) Should English continue to be the official language of Nigeria?
(b) If not, which indigenous Nigerian language should replace it?
(c) Is it necessary to have only one official language?
(d) If not, how many, and which ones?

With regard to question (a), the general desire seemed to be that English should not continue indefinitely as the country's official language. But it was also generally admitted that the logistics for its replacement were difficult to work out. If a target date was to be set, it would be necessary to ensure that the entire load borne by the language was effectively shifted on to another language. This would, in particular, include the use of English as the language of government, legislature and the judiciary. It would also include its use as the medium of instruction at the primary and secondary levels of education. It was generally agreed, on the other hand, that its use at the tertiary level might have to continue indefinitely. The bases of this desire for a change were, of course, nationalism and the quest for authenticity. Every nation, it was felt, should have a national language which sets it apart from other nations.

The U.S.A., Australia and New Zealand would seem to represent a counter-argument, but many Nigerians would insist that these are not really counter-examples. In all three cases, it would be argued, the language had been exported by native speakers of English who had settled and multiplied in the countries almost as if there had been no previous inhabitants. In contrast, a permanent settler population was never on the cards for the British in Nigeria, so English could only be, at best, a second language. On the other hand, that a distinctive language is generally regarded as being crucial to nationhood is attested by Spain and Portugal, and by the Scandinavian countries. There is a high degree of mutual intelligibility between Spanish and Portuguese, to the extent that the two might be regarded as dialects of the same language, and the same is true of Norwegian, Danish and Swedish. In both cases, nationhood demanded the assertion of a separate language.

It is therefore understandable if most Nigerians did not consider themselves as true heirs to the English language in the same way that Americans and Australians do, even while appreciating the many advantages of being proficient in the language. Some way therefore had to be found of retaining English for education, which was considered necessary for development, while a national language, as distinctive as the national flag, was searched for.

This brings us to question (b), and the difficulty in answering it should not be found surprising. It is easy enough for linguists to set up a set of objective criteria for the choice of a national language, and perhaps four such criteria are paramount, namely:

(i) The size of the population already speaking the proposed language. This would presumably determine the amount of effort to be expended on the adoption of the language.

(ii) Current rate of expansion of the language. This would provide an indication of the need that is already felt for the particular language nationally.

(iii) Current state of development of the language. A language to take over from English must, ideally, have developed, to the same extent as English, all the registers of the language necessary for the conduct of national business.

(iv) The current image of the language. Is it a language that everyone is happy to learn? This does not repeat criterion (ii) above which relates to the rate of expansion, for a language may expand, as it were, under duress. To propagate a language in the minimum of time, there must be a certain degree of enthusiasm among the learners. This, in fact, tends to be the criterion most generally emphasized, and hence the occasional calls for a referendum to decide the choice.

An obvious short-list for the honour is the three main languages of the country, whose influence has admittedly been whittled down by the creation of as many as thirty States. But

given the degree of rivalry, sometimes very acrimonious, among the native speakers of these three languages, choosing one of them cannot be expected to be an easy matter. The assumption, not entirely unfounded, is that the winners would come to occupy an excessively advantageous position in the national scheme of things. They would, so it is said, in effect be first-class citizens. In any event, it was not likely that any one of the languages would clearly emerge if the four criteria above were rigorously applied.

The rivalry among the three major languages has, in fact, prompted suggestions that one of the 'minority' languages should be adopted so that the speakers of all the three major languages would be at equal disadvantage. How well such a minority language would fare when put through the four criteria is another matter. Besides, even if the idea were to be accepted in principle, it would merely shift the stampede from the major languages to the more numerous 'minor' languages, many of which have now been promoted to the status of the major languages in their various States.

So, it is urged, why not try a neutral language? Indeed, the call has come from outside the majority language areas to leave well alone and allow the English language to continue indefinitely as the country's official language. But as should be expected, this is not a popular call. So, it is further urged, why not Pidgin? Nigerian Pidgin would conceivably rate higher than any other Nigerian language on the first two of the four criteria stated above. On the third criterion, however, it is not likely to do very well because it has been asked how one would teach a language which has apparently not been standardized and which, it is erroneously claimed, has no grammar. But it must be pointed out that Pidgin is, in fact, the medium of the news bulletin in at least one State of the country, and this use of the language is bound to produce a standardizing influence on the language. Also, of course, there cannot possibly be a language without a grammar; or to put it differently, a language without a grammar is a contradiction in terms. Some people who admit this then go on to claim that the grammar of Pidgin is unstable or 'ad hoc', which boils down to the same complaint as that just considered, namely, that the language has not been standardized.

Perhaps the most telling criticism of Nigerian Pidgin is in two parts. One is that, so far, it is a spoken rather than a written language. The amount of literature in the language is very small though brave attempts have been made by the 'Lagos Weekend' to exploit the literary possibilities of the language. Still, it has to be admitted that there is as yet no generally agreed orthography of the language. While some versions are based on the English orthography, Mafeni (1971) would seem to favour an orthography based on those of the Nigerian indigenous languages, complete with tone-marks and sub-dots. The other part of the criticism has to do with the status of any pidgin language. Pidgins are described as contact languages and therefore by definition are restricted in their communicative range since they are supposed to supplement every speaker's mother tongue. It is when a pidgin becomes creolized that it becomes elaborated and stretched to perform all the functions of a mother tongue. It is not known how many monolingual speakers of Nigerian Pidgin there are, if in fact there are any. For such people and the community in which they live, it means that Nigerian Pidgin has creolized. But it is also the case that many Nigerian bilinguals claim Pidgin to be their first language, meaning not only the first to be acquired temporally, but also the more dominant of their two (or more) languages. What all of this suggests is that 'Nigerian Pidgin' has evolved from being a purely descriptive technical term into a proper name. A very careful examination of this whole question is contained in Elugbe and Omamor (op. cit.).

As for the fourth criterion, Nigerian Pidgin fares not much better. The language has always been regarded as the poor relation of English. In the mouths of several English-speaking Nigerians, it has become the language either of familiarity or of comic discourse. It is paradoxical that while it would be the easiest language to propagate in Nigeria, it is the language taken least seriously. In addition, more militant nationalists would prefer a more complete break with English than that provided by Pidgin.

Technically, though, there could be another reservation. There is a hypothesis that where pidgins and creoles co-exist with their basis, they tend to disappear into the basis (7). If the hypothesis is correct, it would be a matter of time for Nigerian Pidgin to disappear into the English language. Presumably this is because in a society in which a pidgin and its basis are spoken bilingually, the pidgin is regarded as the *basilect* whereas the basis is regarded as the *acrolect*. With increasing education, the acrolect, or at least the mesolect, is acquired by more and more people and the stigma of using a basilect increasingly avoided. Whatever may be the validity of this hypothesis, we may note that the co-existence of English and Krio in Sierra Leone does not appear to threaten the survival of Krio; but then some may say that this only proves that pidgins are more vulnerable in such situations than creoles.

Clearly, the sociolinguistic situation was found to be a complex one. One aspect of the discussion therefore turned on strategies; should a national language be decided in one fell swoop, or should the ground be prepared for it to emerge over a number of years? Professional linguists, more conscious than others of the intricacies of the subject matter, counselled the latter, and their writings have had a profound influence on the national language policy which finally saw the light of day in 1977, and was revised in 1981. While the policy avoids the question of a successor to English as the official or national language, it addresses the issues of a more balanced bilingualism in the country, one which would ensure the use of the mother tongue or the language of the immediate community at critical stages in the process of education. For pre-primary education, the policy stipulates that (p.10):

> 'the medium of instruction will be principally the mother-tongue or the language of the immediate community.'

As for the primary school, the same document goes on to state (p.13):

> 'Government will see to it that the medium of instruction in the primary school is initially the mother tongue or the language of the immediate community and, at a later stage, English.'

At the secondary level, the document (p.17) elevates the Nigerian languages to the status of 'core subjects' alongside Mathematics and English.

For the first time, we have a government policy spelling out the position of English within the educational system and adumbrating a role-sharing between it and the country's indigenous languages. What is even more spectacular, the North and South are at last united in a common policy.

A second epoch-making policy decision affecting the status of the English language in Nigeria is to be found in the country's 1979 constitution. Hitherto, English had been the language of the legislature all over the country, though some experimental steps had been taken in the North to replace it with Hausa. But the legislatures had been suspended in 1966 and replaced with a series of military administrations for thirteen years. At the end of this period, in 1979, the military government was anxious to lay a solid foundation for the re-activation of a democratic parliamentary government, and in order to widen participation in the legislatures as much as possible, it was enshrined in the new constitution that Yoruba, Igbo and Hausa should, as soon as appropriate arrangements had been made, also serve as alternative languages of business to English in the National Assembly. The intention, clearly, was that the State legislators would take the cue from the centre. Unfortunately, the reactivation of the legislature turned out to be short-lived, for in four short months, another military government was in control of the country. The hope, all the same, was that whenever a civilian government was restored in the country, for as long as the language provision in the country's constitution is not amended, the use of the country's indigenous languages in the legislature would gradually gather momentum. A possible end-result would be the eventual replacement of English at the centre with a national language (possibly after an interregnum of the three major languages) and the use of the regional lingua francas in the State Assemblies.

English would thus have a diminished role in national affairs. Would it still be a second language? Strictly speaking, as soon as it ceases to be the country's official language (however long that may take) it also ceases to be the country's second language. Yet it may survive as more than a conventional foreign language for much longer. For one thing, the requirement of English as a condition of entry to the country's tertiary institutions will take a very long time to change. For another, Nigerian literature of English expression has already become part of the national heritage, and the tradition may well continue long after the language has been dis-established.

We may now turn to the other two questions earlier posed, namely, whether it is necessary to have only one official language, and if not, what should be the country's official languages. Attention has often been drawn to countries like Canada and Switzerland which seem to have made a success of operating more than one official language. Without going into too much detail here, it can be said that replacing English with one indigenous language is problematic enough. Replacing it with three is only likely to compound the problems in terms of logistics and costs. Politically also, it may be counterproductive. If the basis for seeking a national language is to establish a linguistic rallying force at the national level, the adoption of three national languages may well prepare the ground for an eventual division of the country into three. Developments even in Canada and Switzerland would seem to bear out the validity of this fear. In other parts of Europe, too, separatist movements often make a great point of the linguistic argument. In the Nigerian situation, therefore, the combination of a national language with regional lingua francas would appear to be the best compromise, balancing the centripetal and centrifugal forces.

C. **Programmes and projects:**

Having discussed the agencies which were responsible for the implantation and development of the English language in Nigeria and the various policies pursued by these agencies, it is time to examine the programmes and projets by means of which the agencies sought to give effect to these policies, even when such policies were not explicitly stated.

The overarching programme is, of course, to be found within the educational system. For historical completeness, we may recall that the first attempts at institutionalizing the teaching of English had been made by a number of Efik entrepreneurs in Calabar in the eighteenth century. These, as we have said, were *ad hoc* attempts made to meet the needs of the moment rather than far-sighted programmes and projects (8).

(i) *Primary Schools*

With the introduction of British-type schools by the missionaries in the middle of the nineteenth century, some thought necessarily had to be given to English education. Yet we have no record of a clearly thought-out programme stating, for example, the level of proficiency envisaged at the end of the primary and secondary levels, nor do we have any explicit statement of the assumptions underlying the training of the teachers of English in the elementary and teacher-training colleges first established by the missionary societies. Only two facts can be clearly established. The first is that the elementary schools admitted children who had had absolutely no prior knowledge of the English language. The other is that the products of the secondary grammar schools were expected to be as proficient in the language as the products of the British grammar schools. It would have been helpful to be able to see how the missionary educational authorities approached this daunting task. Their thinking can only be gleaned today from the curriculum that they established.

Little concession was, in fact, made to the linguistic background of the children arriving on their first day at the elementary schools, and the curriculum imported from Britain was minimally tampered with. Even the text-books were imported from Britain. But of course it would have been impossible to take no notice at all of the fact that the children were learning the English language from scratch at school. Moreover, the missionaries could not have been unaware that a similar situation had been encountered elsewhere in the British empire - notably in India. So, classroom practice was informed by a certain amount of theory and precedence.

Universally, language-learning in the nineteenth century and the early decades of the twentieth was dominated by two main ideas: traditional grammar (together with the associated grammar and translation method) and structural linguistics (together with the associated direct method). Traditional grammar presented a notional definition of grammatical categories and, perhaps even more important for a foreign or second language situation, paid no attention to the spoken language. It was prescriptive in orientation and held up the performance of established *writers* as models. The ultimate models were the famous Latin authors.

A language-learning programme based on this model necessarily emphasized the learning of the grammar of the language and the imitation of the models presented. As in some other parts of the world - particularly in foreign language situations - the model encouraged the grammar and translation method. Obviously, this was not easily practicable in situations where the mother tongue had not been reduced to writing or where there was no homogeneous mother tongue; but this only made the method more laborious in such situations.

At the beginning, therefore, the teaching of English was (a) grammar-oriented and (b) concerned with written rather than oral models, and these were to remain notable characteristics of the enterprise for several decades. Perhaps the claim that the teaching was grammar-oriented needs further elaboration, since all language-learning must necessarily be grammar-oriented. Learning a language, after all, is nothing less than internalizing the grammar of the language. But during the period under consideration, the grammar of a language was defined as a written account of the language, something to be found on the pages of a book. The rules of grammar were memorized to mediate performance in the language. Obviously, the learning was bound to be laborious, but at the same time, in the best cases, quite thorough. But the fact remains that what was learnt was largely literary English, or *sensu* Ubahakwe (1974), 'bookish English.'

With the rise of modern structural linguistics signalled by Sapir's (1921) and Bloomfield's (1933) publications early in the twentieth century, the focus in language study - and therefore, language learning - shifted from written data to spoken data, from literary models to the speech of ordinary native speakers of the language. Languages now had to be described in their own terms, and notional definitions gave way to empirical, scientific, ones. Behaviourism dominated the intellectual climate of the age, and it was thus inevitable that the grammar and translation method of language learning should give way to the direct method which simultaneously emphasized the primacy of speech and the view of language as a behaviour to be learnt to the point of automaticity.

The underlying assumption for the direct method is that there is only one way of learning a language, and that is the way the mother tongue is learnt. For the effective learning of a second or foreign language, therefore, the conditions in which the mother tongue is learnt must be simulated as closely as possible - i.e. by intense exposure to the primary linguistic data. Course books had to be written with all these assumptions in mind.

A fair question to ask is whether in fact the direct method was ever given a fair chance in Nigeria. It is an expensive method relying for good results on an intensive use of technology - a good language laboratory with tapes and films. It is very unlikely that there was a single school in the entire country which had such facilities. In the circumstances, exposure to the language was confined to the classroom in which the only audio-visual aid in most cases - the teacher - was hardly a model to be recommended. It should be recalled that this was the time leading up to national independence when schools were mushrooming and the quality of teachers plunging. At any rate, in the perception of the political leaders, the priority was science, not language education, and the link between the two was either not seen or ignored.

On the face of it, as already remarked, it is hardly surprising that the products of the grammar and translation method of the first three or four decades of the twentieth century should be regarded as being superior to those of the direct method. But we should be careful not to ascribe too much to the method in either case. The most important input to the grammar and translation method is, quite clearly, the intellectual capacity of the learner. But this was precisely what was considered irrelevant under the direct method, which assumes that there is little, if any, correlation between intelligence and language learning. But then, having made that assumption, it requires that something else should be put in the place of intelligence - and that is intensive exposure. During the direct method era in Nigeria, therefore, the English language learner may be described as having fallen between two stools. He was encouraged to abjure the intellectual processes of the old method while not being given the empowerment that is vital to the success of the new.

One salutary by-product of the era of the direct method in the nineteen fifties and sixties was the work done by linguists on contrastive studies between English and various Nigerian languages (cf Tomori,(1967); Afolayan, (1968); Banjo, (1969)). At the height of the era of structural linguistics, it came to be recognized that not only the quantity but also the quality of primary linguistic data is important in the second language learning situation. Thus the data, it was pointed out, should emphasize those aspects in which the grammar of the mother tongue differed from that of the target language. The various contrastive studies strongly influenced the course books being produced and ultimately classroom activity.

The truth is that both methods have important contributions to make to a successful process of language learning. The learning of a second language cannot be a mere replication of that of the mother tongue. In the former, an intellectual process is necessarily involved, because one language is being learnt in the context of another. Such an activity is bound to prod the intellect of any normal human being. He is bound to begin to notice the ways in which the target language is like his mother tongue and how, in other respects, it is not. The learner in such a situation is a practising contrastive analyst, formulating an approximative system to explain the data available to him at every stage. In an important sense, success in learning the language depends on the superiority of the approximative systems thus formulated.

Yet a second language is learnt to be spoken with a certain degree of fluency which arises from confidence; and practice makes perfect. Exposure to data of the right quantity and quality is therefore also crucial. In the absence of the proper machinery for implementing the direct method, many schools in fact fell back on the older method while according a nodding recognition to the direct method by forbidding pupils, on pain of punishment, to speak an indigenous language in the school premises.

Meanwhile, the ideas of Noam Chomsky, first set out in his *Syntactic Structures* (1957) were producing a profound effect on syntactic theory. Structural linguists had reacted - in some cases, over-reacted - to traditional grammarians' monolithic concept of languages by asserting that every language was *sui generis* and that each language differed almost infinitely from every other language. Such a view unfortunately obscured the universal properties of every language, and one of Chomsky's initial outstanding contributions to the philosophy of language was precisely the distinction he made between the universal and idiosyncratic properties of every natural language. The implications of this for contrastive studies is obvious. Its implications for the production of course materials with regard to grading and sequencing are equally clear.

But Chomsky's even greater contribution lies in the fact that his model of linguistic description contained an inherent hypothesis of language acquisition. In place of the prevailing empiricist and behaviourist approach, he posited a rationalist view - a revolutionary one which claims that the mother tongue is acquired not through a process of intensive learning but as a result of a simple choice of the optimal grammar that explains the primary linguistic data. So revolutionary was this concept that it was greeted initially with cynicism, or even hostility. But Chomsky (1985) argues his case quite convincingly on the basis of a rationalist philosophy which assumes that every normal human being, at the appropriate stage of maturation and given the necessary exposure to the primary linguistic data, is programmed by nature to speak a language, much as the individual is programmed to crawl and walk at the appropriate stages of development.

Important questions are raised by Chomsky's theory for second-language learning. To what extent are individuals programmed to acquire more than one language? Is there an upper limit to the number of languages that can be so acquired? Answers to these questions have been attempted (cf Banjo, 1970a;1975;1988) and available evidence would seem to suggest that whereas the mother tongue is *acquired* (in the way suggested by Chomsky), subsequent languages are *learnt* (though not quite in the way assumed by the traditionalists or the structuralists.).

It seems reasonable to assume that there is a higher degree of consciousness involved in learning a second (or foreign) language than in acquiring the mother tongue, hence the necessity for different verbs to describe the activity in each case. The innate predisposition (or *faculte de langauge)* which Chomsky posits may no longer be very active after the acquisition of the mother tongue, but we may assume that it does not disappear altogether. It rather enables the individual, in learning subsequent languages, tacitly to recognize what Chomsky describes as formal and substantive universals. His learning is thus focused on the idiosyncratic properties of the target language, and part of his difficulty arises, as correctly diagnosed by the structuralists, from transfers from the mother tongue.

Contrastive analysis will offer amelioration, but again, not quite in the way suggested by the structuralists. There are, indeed, two variants of the hypothesis of contrastive analysis - the weak one, and the strong one. The strong one, favoured by the structuralists, assumes that every learning point will pose a great and equal amount of difficulty to the learner since languages 'vary infinitely.' On this view, the learner is constantly on a minefield, so to speak. The weak variant, however, is used diagnostically, to explain the errors that are made in the course of learning, more than in confidently predicting each and every error or difficulty.

It is also possible that the distinction between deep structure and surface structure made by Chomsky is relevant in the preparation of course books for second or foreign language learning. Languages are more likely to be alike in their deep (and more abstract) properties than in their surface (or more concrete) ones. It is thus possible to predict a hierarchy of difficulties.

Altogether, transformational-generative grammar has not affected classroom practice in Nigeria as much as it should. This is largely because old habits die hard. Even though there are many people who have the competence to produce appropriate course books in a transformational-generative format, the curriculum handed down by the government hardly makes the production of such books viable. The situation has not been helped either by the introduction of the continuous assessment system, which compels a slavish following of the centrally-produced syllabus.

Meanwhile, as we have already seen, the country's constitution provides that English should become the medium of instruction at a 'later stage' of primary education. The switch is in fact commonly made at the end of the third year. However, the condition in most primary schools is such that teaching in English is heavily interlaced with the mother tongue right up to the final year of the primary school.

Hitherto, there have been three different approaches to the teaching of the English language at the primary school level. One is that typified by such private schools as the Corona schools and the Staff Schools of some of the universities. The provision in the constitution does not really apply to this category of schools because the children have already acquired the English language before their first day at school. Some of them are native speakers of the language, and those who are not are already bilingual with English dominance. Traditionally, such schools have been run almost exactly like their equivalents in Britain.

The second approach is typified by publicly- funded schools which have taken the decision to go 'straight for English' by using English as the medium of instruction throughout the school. A course book appropriately titled 'Straight for English' was adopted by some of such schools, and it may not be an accident that they were predominant in the North, where attitudes to English had remained more puristic than in the South. The population of such schools is more linguistically heterogeneous than in the Corona Schools, and some at least of the children must have felt thrown in at the deep end, at least for the first year. The likelihood of supplementation with Hausa, given the status of that language in the North, cannot also be ruled out. The aim in going 'straight for English' is, obviously, to give the children a head start.

The third approach is the more general one in the country. Even before the provision in the national policy on language in education, it was the approach that had been favoured for more than a century. Two questions arise in connection with this practice of switching over. The first is why it should ever have been contemplated in the first place. Teaching throughout the primary level in the children's mother tongue was certainly a more natural alternative. The switch to English half-way through must have been motivated by the proprietors' desire to produce English-speaking bilinguals by the end of primary education. It must be remembered that for a number of decades, primary education was, in fact, the only form of education available in the country. The second question is : what steps were taken to ensure that the change-over to English as the medium of instruction was realistic? What was the degree of competence and proficiency of the pupils at the point of changeover, and how effectively had the curriculum prepared them for it? An examination of the English curriculum over the last century shows only too clearly that the preparation is grossly inadequate. While it may rightly be argued that thousands of children did survive the system and went on to do well at the secondary and tertiary levels, it must be recognized that the system has also produced a staggering amount of wastage. The English language has been the undoing of many an otherwise bright Nigerian child, and even many of those who did survive had indelible scars to show for it.

If the practice was defensible at the beginning, it is much less so at a time when the secondary and tertiary tiers of education have been more or less fully developed and when the First Leaving Certificate is no longer a passport to any but menial jobs in the country. Yet the national policy on language in education as recently as 1981 still endorsed the practice but significantly is unable to stipulate the exact time of changeover.

Meanwhile, English language-related problems have surfaced, as a result of this practice, at the secondary and tertiary levels, and we shall see later the various attempts made to remedy the situation. Unfortunately, these attempts are made at the secondary and tertiary levels when in fact the root cause ought to have been tackled at the primary level. The point is that if there is an indigenous language (mother tongue for most, language of immediate community for the rest) found viable for the first two or three years of primary education, there is no reason why that same language cannot be used throughout primary education. Admittedly, additional work would be required to produce teaching materials in such a language, but that is not an impossible task, as the Ife Six Year Primary Project has amply confirmed (9).

But it may be argued that the Ife project took place in a linguistically homogeneous area of the country and that, in addition, Yoruba, the language of the area, is in any case one of the most developed indigenous languages in the country. This only shows, however, that the national policy, even as it is couched, will be easier to implement in some parts of the country than in others. The problems of linguistically heterogeneous classes have to be solved anyway, and if they can be solved to make the present official policy work, additional effort can bring about a successful replication of the Ife project with resultant rich dividends at the secondary and tertiary levels.

But there is an important assumption that we should not lose sight of. English in Nigeria is a second rather than a foreign language. As a second language, it is expected that it is widely spoken in the country. The teaching of it should therefore be expected to receive considerable reinforcement outside the classroom. But this leads us into a vicious circle: as a result of inefficient teaching, the quality of external reinforcement is judged to be inadequate, and this inadequate reinforcement at the same time perpetuates ineffectual teaching. By the same token, improved teaching in schools would raise the level of performance generally in the country, and this in turn would produce a desirable backwash effect in the classroom.

Something further should be said about Nigerian children who are already English-speaking on their first day at school. In many cases, they are even monolingual, and for the rest, bilingual with English dominance. This is obviously the breed that Mazrui (1975) has referred to as 'Afro- Saxons.' What is the explanation for this phenomenon?

Three factors inextricably bound together have been at work. The practice would appear to have started in the Corona and such other schools, and in the Staff School of the University of Ibadan which was established soon after the foundation of the university as a College of the University of London in 1948. The staff of the college at that time were very predominantly British with a small admixture of English-speaking members from Europe and Australia. The Staff School was founded for the benefit of such staff and was in fact one of the strong selling points of the new University College to prospective staff abroad. The school was therefore run from the beginning on the assumption that the children were all native speakers of English. However, the few Nigerian members also sent their children to the school and such children had hardly any difficulty because some of them had been born in Britain while their fathers were studying there, and in any case, the university college, which was fully residential, was an English-speaking community *par excellence*. So, from the beginning, the Nigerian children attending the school were either monolingual speakers of English (whether or not to refer to them as native speakers of English is a moot point (cf Davies,1991) or bilingual with English dominance (10).

The case of Corona-type schools is not much different. Nigeria never had a British settler population, but all the same, the British colonial officers, scattered all over the country but more concentrated in Lagos, and British nationals in the mercantile houses have always needed primary schools for their children who were generally sent later to boarding schools in Britain for their secondary education. Some affluent members of the Nigerian English-speaking elite also took advantage of providing quality education for their children and even imitated their British friends to the point of sending their own children, too, to boarding schools in Britain for secondary education.

The second factor was the growing incidence of marriages across ethnic lines among Nigerians, particularly in the case of those who had studied abroad and met their future partners there. In most of such cases, English inevitably became the language of the family and the first language of their offspring. Naturally, such couples sought admission for their children in English-speaking schools, and when later the International School was established at the University of Ibadan, it became possible for the products of these schools to proceed to a secondary school very much resembling the British Public School.

The third factor was the anxiety by many parents of various backgrounds, but with enough resources, to give their children a head start in life. In some cases, it was necessary to send the children to English-speaking nurseries for a couple of years before sending them to one of these elite primary schools. Generally speaking, this was one way in which the English-speaking elite sought to perpetuate itself, and also one way in which the English language has contributed to social stratification in the country.

The breed of 'Afro-Saxons' thus produced by the system can best be described as being bi-cultural with English dominance and do all they can to keep in tune with the culture of Britain by making annual pilgrimages to that country.

(ii) *Secondary Schools*

The medium of instruction in Nigerian secondary schools is, and always has been, English, and one of the reasons sometimes given for the changeover to English as the medium of instruction before the end of primary education is that it is necessary for the pupils to arrive at the secondary school well able to take full advantage of the teaching there.

The missionary societies favoured boarding schools (cf C.M.S. Grammar School, Lagos, and, for teacher-training, Hope Waddell Institute, Calabar, St. Andrew's College, Oyo, and Wesley College, Ibadan), though there were one or two notable exceptions such as the Methodist Boys' High School, and Baptist Academy, both in Lagos, which were day schools. Later, when the government came to participate in offering secondary education, it also established King's College and Queen's College, Lagos, as predominantly boarding schools. Now, whatever the educational benefits of a boarding school education - and they are generally held to be many and notable - there is no denying the fact that the system provided the proprietors with an opportunity of building up the pupils' proficiency in the English language. As boarding life was also patterned generally on the British practice, some might say that they also provided a ready means of assimilation by the pupils to the British culture.

Some of the boarding schools were, indeed, more liberal than others. In some, it was a mortal sin to be heard speaking an indigenous Nigerian language within the precincts of the school; others made no such unnatural laws but rather relied on the intensity of the exposure of the pupils to situations in which English was inevitably the medium. It must be remembered that these early boarding schools drew pupils from all over the country, and therefore the language of all corporate school activities had to be English. A good many of the secondary grammar schools later opened between the beginning of the twentieth century and national independence in 1960 used these older schools as models, providing boarding facilities for some, if not all of their pupils. The strong emphasis on communal living thus brought about provided considerable reinforcement for classroom teaching of English. The creative uses of the language were also encouraged, and school magazines, debating societies and the production of plays became the established features of a good secondary grammar school.

But it must be added that the schools also tended to be rather well equipped, with well-stocked libraries. Even more important, enrolment to many of them was deliberately kept low. For example, Igbobi College, founded in 1932, still had, twenty-five years later, a total pupil enrolment of just about 120, practically all of them boarders.

The approach of independence, however, affected the secondary grammar schools no less than it did the primary schools. The expansion at this level took two forms. The first was the increased enrolments in the existing schools and the founding of more schools, this time by the cumulative efforts of local communities and private individuals. Standards inevitably dropped as the majority of the new schools were either entirely day schools providing minimal communal life to their pupils, or else caricatures of the older, established boarding schools. To worsen matters, from the point of view of the learning of the English language, the prevailing nationalistic mood dictated that too much importance should not be attached to performance in the language, anyway.

The other form that the expansion took was a radical re-thinking of the concept of secondary education itself. Up to the advent of regional governments at the end of the first half of the century, secondary education had been synonymous with grammar school education or the more specialized teacher education. The government of the Western Region now decided - and was soon followed by that of the Eastern Region - to establish secondary modern schools, partly in order to take the pressure off the grammar schools, and partly to create a new labour force of artisans. The experiment is now generally regarded as a monumental disaster, not because there was anything wrong with the philosophy, but because the schools were even more poorly funded than the new generation of grammar schools, whose poor relations they were soon seen to be. For the brief period that the schools lasted, many products came out barely more literate in English than they went in, and in any case soon reverted to near-total illiteracy. Since there were more secondary modern schools than grammar schools, at least in the southern parts of the country, the products of these schools must have contributed significantly to the general feeling which prevailed in the years immediately following national independence that the standards, not only of English, but of education generally, were falling. At any rate, by the end of the first decade of independence, the secondary modern schools had been consigned to oblivion and the alternative idea of comprehensive schools had also been experimented with and dropped. Another decade further on, the country was trying to operate a national policy on education which brought together all the previous philosophies. The first three years of secondary education were to be comprehensive in all but name, offering both academic and vocational education. At the end of this period, there was to be a parting of the ways, with the more academically-inclined pupils going on to three years of senior secondary education while the rest went into various types of vocational schools. Again, the idea is highly commendable, but it remains to be seen whether, in the grips of a deep recession, the economy of the country will permit anything like a satisfactory implementation in the foreseeable future.

One of the steps taken to arrest the perceived fall in standards of English in the secondary grammar schools in the early sixties was to take a critical look at the English language paper in the School Certificate Examination. A former Registrar of the West African Examinations Council and author of a successful English course series, D.W. Grieve, was commissioned to produce a report. The Grieve Report (1964) was flawed in a number of ways (cf Banjo,1967) and in any case did little to remove the impression that many candidates were passing the English paper at the credit level whose proficiency in the language clearly left a great deal to be desired[11].

The International Panel on the English language Paper of the West African Examinations Council (WAEC) met a number of times to consider the situation and made two important observations on the format of the School Certificate English language paper. The first related to the methods of testing comprehension, syntax and lexis. Because of phenomenal increases in the numbers of candidates, WAEC had been compelled to introduce the 'multiple choice' system of testing, whereby candidates had to identify, from a set of items, the appropriate one to answer a given question. This system, it has been pointed out, laid itself open to guess-work on the part of the candidates. But more important, *knowing* the answer to a question was quite different from *recognizing* the answer to the same question. This criticism applied as well to the syntax questions, where such relations as synonymy and antonymy were tested, as to the test of comprehension, which took the form of Cloze texts in which gaps in a passage were to be filled in by candidates with words from a set of words provided. The former tests of precis and comprehension, it was felt, constituted a superior test of proficiency. Of course, they were also more expensive to administer.

The other observation was that the Oral English test really ought to be an integral part of the English test instead of being optional. What was worse, a candidate who passed the Oral English test had the grade entered on his certificate, but no mention of it was made on the certificate of anyone who took the test but failed. There was a sharp disagreement here between the members of the International Panel and the experts from WAEC's Tests Development and Research Office (TEDRO). The former's argument was in two parts. First, they argued that the spoken skills of the language were as important as the literacy skills in a second language situation, and pointed out that the intelligibility of the language, even within the country, might be jeopardised if advantage was not taken of the standardizing influence of WAEC's Oral English test. As it was, because the spoken skills were not tested as part of the English language paper, no attempt was made to teach them in most schools.

Furthermore, they argued that progress in developing the literacy skills of reading and writing was bound to be adversely affected by the lack of a solid foundation in the skills of oracy. They insisted that the grammar of a language is more naturally internalized through listening and speaking than through writing and reading, and that failure in oracy is inevitably transferred to literacy. At the more mechanical level, they drew attention to the plethora of spelling mistakes which originate from faulty pronunciation.

The TEDRO experts did not really attempt to counter these arguments. Rather, they based their own argument on the results of experiments purportedly carried out elsewhere which, they claimed, showed a high degree of correlation between a candidate's performance in the test of literacy skills and that of oracy. The members of the international panel remained deeply sceptical of these experimental findings but could do nothing to make the TEDRO experts - and consequently, WAEC -budge.

Further discussion, however, suggested that WAEC's real problem was the costs that would be incurred in applying the Oral English test on every candidate taking the English language paper -which, in effect, meant *every* candidate taking the School Certificate examination. The Oral English test is in two parts. The first is a test of comprehension, in which candidates listen to recorded material and then answer 'multiple choice' questions on it. The other is a test of production in which every candidate individually faces the examiner and performs a reading task, followed by a short oral composition. The production test takes between ten and fifteen minutes per candidate, and if it were to be made compulsory for every candidate, would involve enormous costs. But even if the financial resources were available and the time could be arranged, there was the insuperable problem of adequately qualified examiners. It would require a large pool of examiners - possibly at least one from every school - to make compulsory testing work. The alternative of recording all the candidates on this test and then having the taped performances marked centrally by a small group of examiners was also examined, and it was estimated that, even then, several miles of tape would be required. Besides, recording of candidates at some of the centres might be problematic, even with the use of batteries.

So the real unanswerable argument was that of feasibility. No one could really doubt the advantages of having the spoken skills properly taught in schools - because compulsorily tested in the School Certificate examination - both as a necessary foundation for the literacy skills and because of obvious sociolinguistic needs. At the same time, TEDRO never proved with local statistics the presumed correlation between test performances in oracy and literacy. The matter seems likely to become live again, however, because Oral English is now prescribed in the national curriculum which all secondary schools are compelled to follow in accordance with the national policy on education. One feature of the curriculum is that there will be continuous assessment, and this will presumably apply also to oral work. If indeed oral work is to be tested through continuous assessment, it would remove the logistical problem of organizing a massive test at the end of every school year. It would, in fact, be a more satisfactory way of testing these skills. But it will not have solved the problem of qualified personnel. One may, indeed, wonder just how the schools are coping in this respect.

The point that emerges is the need for professionalising the English language teaching profession in Nigeria, and another pointer in the same direction is the Ife Six Year Primary Project. If the language is to be taught in such a way as to have a high surrender value, many linguists argue, it has to be taught by professionals at all levels. Meanwhile, the government, with the aid of the British Council, mounted an improvement project in 1987 for English language teaching in secondary schools. The aim was to familiarize the teachers with the latest methods of the teaching of English as a second langauge, and the target appears to be have been all those involved in teaching the subject.

The value of this project is, however, likely to be adversely affected by the fact that not all those who teach the language in fact have the requisite background. While some have degrees in English with emphasis on literature, others simply possess an Arts degree, which is often wrongly felt to be adequate for the purpose.

However, a fair assessment of the current situation must await a fuller implementation of the present national policy on education, as a result of which secondary education leading up to the School Certificate Examination is now to take six years instead of the previous five. It would also be necessary to see the ingenuity of the school authorities in ensuring that the English language syllabus is effectively covered.

Significantly, however, there have been strong demands for English grammar to be more explicitly taught in schools. But first, we may ask, what seems to be the goal of English language teaching in the secondary school? As at the primary level, it is possible to define the goal both educationally and sociologically. Educationally, the goal at the primary level is, as we have seen, to make it possible for the language to become the medium of instruction before the end of that level. Sociologically, however - and here the goal seems never to have been clearly defined - the aim is to enable the pupil to function within reasonable limits as a bilingual (the missionaries would, no doubt, have related this to the production of competent interpreters). Ideally, those limits should then be clearly set out.

At the secondary level, the educational goal is obviously to reinforce the pupil's ability to profit from secondary education both in and out of the classroom and, in a number of cases, to furnish him with the linguistic tools necessary for the pursuit of a tertiary education. Sociologically, the aim should be to enable the products of secondary education to function effectively in all the situations in which the English language is used in the country. Such domains of use have been referred to by many linguists (cf Bamgbose, (1971); Akere, (1982)), but will briefly be referred to again later.

It would be more correct to say, however, that the teaching going on in secondary schools is determined entirely by the requirements of the School Certificate examination, which indeed may be able to measure success in relation to the educational goal but is unable to test in terms of the sociological goal to any meaningful degree. It is therefore argued that the only effective way to change classroom practice is to change the School Certificate syllabus, especially in this case where the oral aspects of the langauge - the most important aspects sociologically- are not tested.

The problem is a fundamental one, and it has to be accepted that there is no way of testing all the English language skills that a pupil is expected to have acquired in the course of secondary education. If English were a foreign language in the country, that aim would have been more easily realizable. At the other extreme, in a mother tongue situation, no one would dream of embarking on such a venture, the goal of testing being exclusively an educational one, while at the same time, teaching for acculturation purposes does go on all the time and is strongly reinforced by the larger society. The second language situation, as we would expect, shares some of he features of both the foreign language situation and the mother tongue situation. As in the mother tongue situation, it is assumed that a great deal of learning of the language goes on outside the classroom, and this presumably explains why in Nigeria the goal of testing is virtually exclusively educational. But the second language situation is like the foreign language situation in that the pupils are bilingual and therefore need to have the domains of use more clearly defined for them than in the mother tongue situation.

(iii) *The University:*
The University of Ibadan, the oldest university in Nigeria, was established in 1948 as a college of the University of London, and one feature that the college shared with its parent university was the absence of any further training in the skills of the English language at this tertiary level. Fortunately, in the first two decades of the institution's life, this did not matter, for the students combined a sound academic background with very high motivation. By the second half of the 1960's, however, the situation had changed to such an extent that the institution, then the four-year old autonomous University of Ibadan, felt that something should be done, particularly about the slow reading habits of the students of its Faculty of Arts.

There could be no doubt that the slow reading habits exhibited by the students of the Faculty of Arts were but symptoms of a more serious linguistic malaise. However, the university set out in the first place to treat these symptoms. With the help of the Rockefeller Foundation of America, it opened the doors of its Reading Centre in 1966 to the students of the Faculties of Arts and Education and offered training in faster and more efficient reading. At a time when the reading speed of the average American undergraduate was estimated to be about 400 words per minute, that of the average Ibadan Arts undergraduate was found to be as low as 176. It is to the credit of the Reading Centre that this low average was raised to about 350 as a result of one session's remedial work.

No sooner was training in reading remediation begun at the Reading Centre, however, than other underlying language deficiencies began to reveal themselves. Gradually, the Centre expanded its activities to include training in the other language skills - in writing, in listening comprehension and in speaking. Eventually, the Centre's name became a misnomer and was changed to the Department of Language Arts, offering not only courses in the remediation of language skills but also developmental ones in those skills, as well as in the academic study of the skills (12).

If the British Universities did not consider any further training in English necessary for their undergraduates, who were armed with passes at the credit level in the various School Certificate examinations, the American universities thought differently, prescribing the Freshman English course for all their undergraduates. Unlike the University of Ibadan, the University of Nigeria, Nsukka, founded in 1960, was more oriented towards the American than the British university system, and partly under its influence, all the other Nigerian universities were becoming more eclectic, finally substituting the unit- credit- course system for the British-type course delivery system and also ultimately changing from a term calendar to a semester one.

Now, all Nigerian universities offer a General Studies programme, at the heart of which lies a developmental course in English. No student may graduate without passing the prescribed General Studies courses. Before these recent efforts, complaints had been rife of low standards of English usage by the students of Nigerian universities as well as by the graduates.

It may well be asked how it is that after some ten years of learning the English language and being taught the other subjects in the same language, many students arrive at the university without the requisite proficiency in the language and graduate without being the models of bilingualism that they ought to be. But the answer should be partly clear from our earlier consideration of the situation at the primary and secondary levels. The state of affairs at the tertiary level is but the cumulative effect of the conditions at the two previous levels.

The situation at the tertiary level would seem to indicate a failure at the secondary level both in educational and sociological terms, and it is necessary to examine how this is so. If English language performance at the tertiary level is not meeting the educational requirements, there can be three possible reasons. One is that not enough candidates obtain the pass at credit level required for university admission, and that therefore the universities are having to admit candidates with passes at lower levels. Although it may be the case that there have been a number of waivers, particularly in favour of very promising science students, it is generally not true that the universities have lowered their admission standards in this regard.

A second possible explanation is that WAEC's own standards have fallen, so that a credit pass is below the actual expectation of the universities. There are many who feel that this is the case. As already remarked, there are also many who consider that the changeover from the previous methods of examining English to the 'multiple-choice' format inevitably brought about a lowering of standards. Many candidates, it is asserted, are getting credit passes without deserving them and would not have got them under the old dispensation. What this calls for is a re-appraisal of the validity and reliability of the present format for measuring linguistic skills and predicting performance. Attention has already been drawn in this book to the difference between testing *knowledge* and testing *recognition*. In addition, by its very nature, 'multiple choice' questions are better able to test the mechanics of a language than the more creative aspects of the candidate's competence and proficiency in the language. Here the old methods of precis/summary and comprehension are superior, though it must be admitted that they are also more expensive to administer. The most reliable paper in the present format, therefore, is the composition one, and many candidates do in fact fare badly in this, only to redeem themselves in the 'multiple choice' paper.

Obviously then, English language examining at the secondary level is in need of reform. But before elaborating on this, let us examine the third possible explanation for the present situation. It is simply that there is poor coordination between the secondary and tertiary levels. By this view, WAEC may have maintained its own standards, but the standards in the universities have risen, so that a credit pass is no longer adequate for university education. The proponents of this view hold that a developmental course in English is a *sine qua non* at the university level to fill the inevitable gap between the secondary and tertiary levels, and the example of the American universities is often cited. If a country in which English is spoken as the mother tongue (though admittedly not by every single citizen) finds it necessary to run a Freshman English course in its universities, how much more desirable, it is argued, for a country in which English is a second language to do the same. The Nigerian universities have come round to this point of view, and the National Universities Commission through its minimum standards requirements has given its stamp of authority.

But it is also necessary to examine the cause of the present dissatisfaction with the Nigerian graduate's performance in English. This can similarly be traced to deficiencies at the secondary level, though the universities themselves should bear part of the blame. As our earlier review suggests, the sudden expansion of secondary education in the years immediately preceding and following national independence made it impossible for the sociological goal of teaching the English language to be met by the secondary schools. The result is that, at the tertiary level, students arrived with a highly restricted range of proficiency in the language, and particularly with the minimum levels of competence in oracy. Up till about 1975 when the universities were very largely residential, it was possible to remedy the situation to some extent. But after that year, the expansion in education had already caught up with the universities themselves, with the number of universities rising from one in the fifties to six in the sixties and to thirteen in the seventies. At this point, the residential idea had had to be largely abandoned in the universities, and what used to be Halls of Residence with a rich communal life had become mere hostels in which the students lived a largely atomistic existence. It then became true to speak of students 'passing through the universities without the universities passing through them.' The tutorial system was at the same time breaking down, and with it, any lively oral exchanges between teacher and student.

Unlike the lower levels, the universities were thought to have no educational goal in English to achieve but were expected to achieve the sociological goal of producing model bilinguals, no matter their areas of specialization. Students were expected during their years at the university to have acquired much practice in the use of English in an extensive range of situations in a community which is a microcosm of the larger society itself. But conditions which made this possible in the fifties and sixties had all but disappeared in the seventies.

But an even more pessimistic view would be to assert that it is too late to attempt to rectify the situation at the tertiary level, anyway. As we have seen, however, some work is being done of both a remedial and developmental nature in the universities. In effect, the universities now admit that they, too, have an educational goal to achieve. They have to ensure that linguistic disabilities do not stand between their students and a successful university career, and some measure of success has been recorded in this direction, though few lecturers, particularly those in the science-based faculties, would allow themselves to be bothered by the quality of their students' performance in English. At any rate, the general studies programme now constitutes an attempt by the universities themselves to draw a base line in English proficiency.

No such effort on the sociological front is observable. The matter lies outside the purview of formal curricula and has to do with the quality of life which a student is made to participate in as a student. Unfortunately, it is the first aspect of university life to suffer when there is under-funding, and one which, like character-training, the universities hope that the students are getting simply by virtue of being students.

The concern in the universities about English language proficiency came at a time when applied linguists were exploring the idea of the teaching of English for special purposes. The English programme within the General Studies course could thus be seen as the teaching of English for academic purposes. Of course, within the major area of English for academic purposes, it would be necessary to recognize sub-areas dealing with English for science, for the social sciences, for the humanities etc. Support has come to the universities from, again, the British Council which, as we have seen, had launched a project at the secondary level. The project at the tertiary level is called the Communication Skills Project (COM-SKIP). This was also inaugurated in 1987, to strengthen the English language component of the general studies programmes in all the conventional universities in the country. Briefly put, the programme seeks to professionalize the teaching of Use of English at this level. The universities were grouped into three zones for the purposes of the project, with zonal headquarters located at Ibadan, Nsukka and Bayero Universities. Suitable staff were identified at each university, and some of them sent to the University of Reading in England to pursue higher studies in the specialized area of English for academic purposes.

Next, the project carried out a series of workshops, as a result of which an optimal syllabus for the Use of English course was fashioned out. In the process, also, an Association of Lecturers of English for Academic Purposes was formed, and future activities planned included the publication of a journal. The ultimate goal of the project is, of course, to locate the training of staff in Nigerian universities where suitable programmes at the Masters and Doctorate levels would be developed for the purpose. A similar project aimed at the universities of technology was subsequently launched and named COMSKIPTECH. The launch of these projects was timely, in view of the requirements for minimum standards in the universities earlier referred to, but their success will depend on adequate funding.

To complete the picture, mention should also be made of the survey of English language teaching earlier made under the auspices of the Ford Foundation in 1966 and reported in Jacobs et al (1966). This survey covered the three tiers of the educational system, unlike the Ife Six Year Primary Project which was directed at the primary level, though with expected dividends at the higher levels; the British Council project aimed at more efficient teaching at the secondary level; and the COMSKIP and COMSKIPTECH at the tertiary level. The government has implemented parts of the Ford Foundation Survey report, and the most significant outcome was the establishment of the National Language Centre which, at the beginning, was placed within the educational services section of the Federal Ministry of Education.

High hopes were entertained for the part to be played by this Centre in raising the standards of teaching the English language within the entire educational system, and thus in meeting both the educational and sociological goals of teaching the language. But in the event, the Centre suffered very slow gestation and, in any case, quite rightly extended its horizons to cover the development of the indigenous languages as well. Indeed, by the time the Centre finally got under way after more than twelve years of planning, the urgent issues of the day had changed, and related, not so much to the teaching of English as to the national language question and mother tongue education. Nevertheless, the Centre has been able to keep up the publication of *Language Teacher*, which deals mainly with English language teaching. Still, many would argue that the Centre's most important contribution to date has been the publication of a quadrilingual dictionary of legislative terms commissioned by the legislative assembly itself in 1983, a few months before the military intervention which occurred at the end of that year and put the project in abeyance for some time.

The Centre has now been merged with the Nigerian Educational Research and Development Centre and there are fears that it may consequently lose not only its distinct identity but the ability to play the important roles envisaged for it by those who have taken part in developing a blueprint for it over a period of some twenty years.

In the chapters following, we shall examine how the various agencies described in this chapter and their policies, programmes and projects, leading first to the implantation and then the survival of the English language in Nigeria, have resulted in changing a people's way of life, obliging them to make a virtue of necessity.

NOTES

1. It is now usual to speak of the period between the establishment of the trading companies and the inauguration of the Southern and Northern Protectorates in 1900 as a period of informal colonization (cf Schmied,1991) or of company rule. The two Protectorates were amalgamated by Lord Lugard in 1914 but in many important respects still differently administered for most of the colonial period.

2. For a discussion of this, see Hancock (1971) briefly summarized below.

3. Such conscious learning need not, of course, take place within a formal educational system (cf Banjo (1993)). An important distinc-

tion has to be made between this variety of English and that spoken by the average product of the primary school.

4. The effect of teaching English to speakers of Pidgin has not been much documented. There are conflicting claims, based on impressionistic assessment, as to whether or not the knowledge of Pidgin facilitates or impedes the learning of English.

5. See also Jibril (1986) and his distinction between Southern English and Hausa English. Jibril also demonstrates that a convergence between the two is already taking place.

6. Jibril (op.cit.) analyses the phonological consequences of the phenomenon.

7. A discussion of this hypothesis in relation to language acquisition is discussed in Banjo (1988).

8. See Forde (1956), quoted in Spencer (1971).

9. The Ife Six Year Project, as the name suggests, was an experiment carried out to find out whether or not teaching all subjects at the primary level in the pupils' mother tongue was more beneficial to the pupils than the prevailing method of switching over to English as the medium of instruction half-way through. The reports on the project indicate that not only did the experimental group do better in all subjects than the control group, but that they did better even in the English examination itself. It is claimed that the superiority was maintained right up to the tertiary level of education.

10. See also Paikeday (1985) in which the author challenges the common definitions of *native speaker* and advocates the substitution of the term *proficient user*.

11. The Grieve Report was, all the same, epoch-making, in that it signalled the beginning of a debate on the need for an endonormative model of English in West Africa. The debate was particularly lively in Nigeria - (cf Walsh(1967)and Salami(1968)). Now, Nigerian linguists generally agree on the concept of Nigerian English and at-

tempts are being made to define the standard in linguistic terms - (cf Ekong(1978),Jibril (1986), Akere (1982), Adetugbo (1977) and Jowitt(1991) among others.

12. The name of the department has been further changed to the Department of Communication and Language Arts, to reflect the further broadening of its concerns.

2

Nigerian Use of English

There is an ambiguity in the title of this chapter which is intended to suggest the ground to be covered. One meaning refers to the situations in which Nigerians use the English language and therefore poses the question: when? In answer to this question, it would be necessary to examine the domains in which the language is used in Nigeria. The other meaning, on the other hand, invites attention to the characteristics of the English language in Nigeria and therefore poses the question: what? In this chapter, we shall try to answer both questions and in the process study the trend set in motion by the agencies, policies, programmes and projects discussed in the last chapter. A third interpretation is, indeed, possible and is a normative one relating to how efficiently Nigerians use the English language. Reference was made in the last chapter to informed opinion on this, and the matter will not be pursued any further in this chapter, the orientation of which will be purely descriptive.

The English language is spoken by about 600 million people in the world, though only half of that number speak it as their mother tongue (Strevens, (1981); Bailey and Gorlach,(1982)). For the 300 million for whom English is not the mother tongue, some of them speak it as a second language, and the rest as a foreign language. This sociolinguistic typology of speakers of English is by now generally well-known and therefore will only be briefly summarized here.

The oldest and original speakers of English as mother tongue are to be found in England and the southern parts of Scotland (where the variety of English spoken is now sometimes referred to as Scots, though originally referred to as Inglis). The language was a by-product of the settlement in those parts of present-day Britain by the Angles, the Saxons and the Jutes in the fifth century A.D..

Before the advent of these Germanic tribes from the European continent, Britain had been inhabited by Celtic-speaking peoples. For more than a thousand years, English was confined to this relatively small geographical area of the world. However, with the 'discovery' of America in 1492 by Columbus and the ensuing transatlantic colonization came the phenomenon of English in the diaspora, and it is a point worth noting that almost simultaneously, English was also making contact with the languages of West Africa as well as of India, though the development of the language in the latter two areas was to be different from that in the American colonies. Subsequent activities of colonization similarly led to the transplantation of English as mother tongue to Australia, New Zealand and South Africa.

In Britain, the United States, Australia, Canada, New Zealand and South Africa, therefore, English functions as the mother tongue; but this is not just because there are people these for whom English is the mother tongue - there are also many people in France or Hong Kong for whom English is the mother tongue - but because the language, additionally, serves as the national language and the official language in those countries, though certain modifications must be made with respect to Canada and South Africa, where English shares the honours with another language. The mother tongue situation is the most natural situation, one in which a language bears the entire burden of social intercourse.

The situation in the former British colonies in Africa, Asia and the West Indies is different, though by no means uniform. There, English has been superimposed as the official language over the indigenous languages (in the case of the West Indies, creoles with English and French bases). Therefore, although there are numerous inhabitants of these countries for whom English is the mother tongue, sociologically, it is a second language both because the great majority of the citizens of those countries learn the language after they have acquired an indigenous language as mother tongue, and because there are domains in the corporate lives of the inhabitants to which the language is irrelevant. For example, life goes on in many rural areas of Nigeria without a word of English being spoken. The more the presence of the government is felt, the more important the English language becomes.

It has become increasingly common to identify the varieties of English spoken and written in second language situations as 'new Englishes. 'It is not easy to see the justification for this neologism in preference to the more technical and certainly less subjective 'English as a second language.' At any rate, 'new Englishes' would seem to suffer from the same kind of semantic vagueness as 'the new world' and 'new countries.' Moreover, the definition of New English given by Platt et al (1984:2) would apply in every detail to English as a second language[1]:

'1. It has developed through the education system. This means that it has been taught as a subject and, in many cases, also used as medium of instruction in regions where languages other than English were the main languages. The degree to which English is used as a medium of education for other subjects varies considerably from nation to nation and from one type of school to another.

2. It has developed in an area where a native variety of English was *not* the language spoken by most of the population. For various reasons... pidgin and creole languages are not considered to be *native varieties of English.*

3. It is used for a range of functions *among* those who speak or write it in the region where it is used. This means that the new variety is used for at least some purposes such as : in letter writing, in writing of literature, in parliament, in communication between the government and the people, in the media and sometimes for spoken communication between friends and in the family. It may be used as a lingua franca, a general language of communication, among those speaking different native languages or, in some cases, even among those who speak the same native language but use English because it is felt to be more appropriate for certain purposes.

4. It has become 'localized' or 'nativized' by adopting some language features of its own, such as sounds, intonation patterns, sentence structures, words, expressions. Usually it

has also developed some different rules for using language in communication.'

Platt et al might well have added that 'New English' or English as a second language is, as a rule, a feature of certain former colonies of Britain which have retained the language and are attempting to come to terms with it in a variety of ways, including downgrading it to the status of a special foreign langauge, but never upgrading it to that of a mother tongue.

Unlike the previous two classifications, English as a foreign language has no sociological underpinning. It operates at the individual rather than corporate level, and one does not need to learn it to be a fully integrated citizen of one's country. Many people learn it in the interest of their profession (e.g. the Turkish ambassador to London, or the Chinese ambassador to the United Nations); others so that they can have a good holiday in Australia or Singapore. Some need just the written form of the language; others only the spoken form; others still, both written and spoken forms of a very limited number of registers.

It is customary to draw attention to a distinction to be made between this sociolinguistic typology and the typology of individual speakers of English though, of course, there are interconnections. A mother tongue speaker of a language is one who has been enveloped in the language from birth and is able to convey his most intimate feelings naturally in the language. He need not even be literate in the language. Such a person, as we have said, need not be resident exclusively in countries where the language is the mother tongue in the sociological sense but anywhere at all. He may even go on to acquire a second language (such as French, if as an Englishman he should decide to settle down in France) and add a foreign language as well.

The typical second language speaker of English, on the other hand, is a bilingual who has acquired his own mother tongue before learning English. His mother tongue obviously does not serve him as an Englishman's in England does. Rather, he is more like the Englishman just considered who has settled down in France and for whom English becomes the language of the home (assuming he does not have a French wife). The mother tongue in a second language situation may be of great cultural importance but is of very limited economic and social value, hence the eagerness with which the English language is learned in all countries where it is the second language.

But there are at least two problems about the term 'second language.' It suggests that it is the second language learnt serially in time, and of course this is true in the great majority of cases. We need, however, to consider the small minority for whom, in fact, the second language is the first language to be acquired serially in time. Examples would be the 'Afro-Saxons,' to whom reference was made earlier, and who, though living in an African country where English is the second language, learn to speak English before, if ever, learning an indigenous language, which in some cases may even be a pidgin or creole.

However, Davies (1991) has even raised questions regarding the appropriateness of referring to people like the Afro-Saxons as native speakers of English[2]. Certainly, their earliest relationship with the language cannot be comparable to that of English children born to English parents and brought up in England. Nevertheless, the fact remains that chronologically, many African children acquire English as their first language. This would seem to suggest the necessity to make a distinction between mother tongue and first language, such that a mother tongue speaker would be equivalent to a native speaker but a first language speaker need not be.

The second problem is that of dominance. By this reading, a second language may be thought to be second in importance to another language to the people who speak it. But in fact, nothing can be farther from the truth. In Nigeria, as in all other true English as a second language situations, English is the dominant language in the bilingual's repertoire. It is the language of social and economic power, and the bilingual's mother tongue (or first language) is generally of secondary importance. This is precisely the state of affairs that many countries in which English is spoken as a second language are worried about, and to which language policies are addressed. In some cases, such as India, English is retained as the official language while another language - one indigenous to the country - is promoted as the national language. In others, such as Zambia, a more radical decision is taken to replace English both as the official language and the national language. In Nigeria, the dominance of English remains largely unassailed, and we have seen how the 1977 national policy on education sought to address the situation.

With well over half a billion speakers, English is clearly the world's most important language today. But to the numerical strength of its speakers must be added the many outstanding uses to which the language is put today - in science and technology, in the arts and in international diplomacy. When therefore Nigeria became independent in 1960, it found - like India and Ghana before it - that perhaps the most important legacy of the years of colonization was the English language. Yet, as we have seen earlier, there was an ambivalence towards the language. Here was a language which provided a window on the world and made rapid development a feasible proposition. At the same time, it was a reminder of an inglorious period of the national history. Clearly, a re-definition of attitudes was called for.

In the last chapter, we saw how both elite and popular attitudes towards the English language had changed between early nineteenth century and mid-twentieth. The prevailing assimilationist attitude of the nineteenth century and the first half of the twentieth gave way in the run-up to national independence to a militantly nationalistic one. But this attitude, as we have seen, took its toll on the general standards of education, to which standards in the English language were inextricably linked. To remedy the situation, integrative motivation which hitherto had inspired higher standards in the language had to be replaced with an equally potent instrumental motivation. The matter was, not unexpectedly, the subject of considerable public debate, and one of the striking images used by the proponents of the universalist attitude was that of a motor car. 'Is Nigeria to give up the use of the motor car,' it was asked, 'because it is a foreign invention?' The wise course, it was urged, was to use the English language to get the work of rapid development done. And just as the prototype motor car had been adapted and modified in different parts of the world, so too had the English language. Moreover, just as certain characteristics define the motor-car, wherever manufactured in the world, so certain properties define the English language wherever in the world it is spoken. Indeed, as we shall see later, the process of adaptation was already on. Amos Tutuola had already stunned the world with his *Palmwine Drinkard* while a generation of creative writers of acrolectal English - represented by Achebe, Soyinka, Clark and others - was also stepping forward.

But if instrumental motivation was to be encouraged in the overall interest of national development, the question of how much English Nigeria needed had to be addressed. Obviously, with regard to English, the country could not possibly convert itself into a mother tongue situation and join countries like the United States of America, Australia and New Zealand. Rather, a better model would be India which, while retaining the English language as its official language, was at the same time planning meaningful roles for its indigenous languages.

The tacit adoption of English as the official language of Nigeria immediately suggests the domains of use of the language. The third point in Platt et al's definition of 'New English' quoted earlier in fact addresses itself to this. If English was to be the language of all official business, it became necessary to spell out, in turn, where such official business might be found. Obviously, it would include the legislature, all government offices, the judiciary and the administration of education. But it must also include such non-governmental domains as commerce and journalism. Still further removed from government business is the use of English in literature and in most formal gatherings. It also serves as a restricted lingua franca.

In answering the question: when? we may in fact set up a cline for the use of English in Nigeria, ranging from domains where only English may be used, at one end, to those in which it is minimally used, if at all, at the other. This, however, is not as easy as it may at first appear, for there are situations in which records must be kept in English but prior spoken transactions may take place in any of the country's indigenous languages. Furthermore, there are many spoken transactions in which code-switching is freely accepted. To further complicate the picture, practice is not uniform throughout the country.

One generalization that can safely be made is that English tends to be the language of official record-keeping rather than of all official spoken transactions. If we take government offices, for example, it is not true that the civil servants spend all day speaking English either to one another or to those coming there to transact business. On the other hand, all records are kept in English - even records of transactions which may have been conducted in another language. The same applies to the judiciary, from the Magistrates courts upwards. The records are kept in English and judgments are also delivered in that language,but part of the proceedings may be in another language translated to the court by interpreters. The situation in the Customary Courts is even more interesting, with the entire proceedings, including the delivery of judgment, taking place exclusively in an indigenous language but the records still kept in English.

As already noted, Hausa in the north has tended to share the status of official language in all but name in many domains with English . This is especially true of the legislature where, in the old Northern House of Assembly, Hausa was introduced alongside English as the medium of debate. Elsewhere, this was one domain in which English was the sole language of debate and of the Hansard. As already noted, however, the 1979 constitution has provided for the use of Yoruba, Igbo and Hausa as additional languages of business in the legislature. It remains to be seen what effect this will have on the production of the Hansard.

Secondary and tertiary education is another domain which calls for the exclusive use of English. All teaching and examining is done in English, as are all corporate activities at these two levels. The present trend is to allow the students to interact informally with one another outside the classroom in any language of their choice. All school records are, of course, kept in English.

English is the language of international commerce, largely in the sense that orders have to be made in English. Here again, we see the importance of English as the language of record-keeping even when transactions are with non-English speaking countries. A good deal of the spoken transactions may, however, be conducted in an indigenous language understood by the parties concerned. Outside international commerce, English may still be the language of record-keeping by the bigger firms but hardly has any place as the language of spoken transaction (written transactions in all cases are in English). At the local market level, English has hardly any place at all, and on occasions when a lingua franca becomes necessary, Pidgin serves the purpose. The ordinary sellers in these markets keep their records for the most part in their heads, but some record may be kept in the indigenous languages as well as in a variety of English.

Any newspaper which aims at national coverage must necessarily publish in English. There are newspapers serving the larger linguistic groups, and Yoruba and Hausa newspapers, for instance, have had a fairly long and distinguished record. No African country is better served with English-medium newspapers than Nigeria, and the scene has been further enriched in recent years by a profusion in all manner of periodicals spanning the whole range from the basilectal to the acrolectal. Nothing better confirms that English is the language of literacy in Nigeria.

At the same time, as previously remarked, the English language is being put to creative uses. This phenomenon will be discussed more fully later, but we may here briefly note that it represents an important aspect of the indigenization of the language in Nigeria, and the final proof that, like Latin before it, the English language has become the property of the entire world.

Even in non-official business, English is dominant as the medium of letter-writing in Nigeria. The pattern is similar to that which we have just been discussing; in bilingual families, where day-to-day interaction is in the mother tongue, all letters between members are written in English. The same is true of close friends who share the same mother tongue. The reason for this, surely, is that the Nigerian bilingual's literacy skills in English far outstrip those in his mother tongue. Indeed, in several cases, such skills in the mother tongue may be practically non-existent. The problems of orthography are just being tackled for many of the Nigerian languages, while in others, existing divergent orthographies are being harmonized.

With regard to the spoken language among bilinguals, the general pattern is for technical or formal discussions to be held in English while informal and intimate ones are held in a common indigenous langauge. Certainly a discussion between two unacquainted Nigerian bilinguals would start off in English. If it then transpired that they in fact shared the same mother tongue, or had the same indigenous Nigerian language in common, the discussion might switch to that other language and proceed through a series of code-switching and language mixing. However, if either or both of them were unwilling to establish rapport between them (perhaps because of social differences) the discussion might continue throughout in English. Language choice between two Nigerian bilinguals who share the same linguistic repertoire is always significant. In the spoken mode, a choice determined by the field and tenor of discourse (*sensu* Enkvist et al 1964) has to be made consciously.

One important fact which emerges from the fore-going discussion is that in Nigeria, the skills of literacy in English are more important than those of oracy. It may be asked whether this has always been so. The phenomenon does, indeed, have a strong historical basis. Before the nineteenth century, Pidgin had more or less served the needs of spoken interactions between the English traders and the local population. The number of people, especially from the late seventeenth century, who spoke English rather than (or in addition to) Pidgin was too small to result in a flourishing English-speaking community, and in any case, the registers of the language that they were proficient in must have been severely limited, being strictly orientated towards the needs of commerce where, indeed, record-keeping was of prime importance. We may also recall that even Antera Duke's writings have come down to us in the form of entries in his diary - i.e. his own personal records, which had possibly been inspired by the records kept by the trading companies. Of course, it must be admitted that there is no way now of judging how much and what kind of English was spoken during this period. But since English was, in fact, a foreign language needed for the specific purpose of commerce, the amount must have been small and, if spelling is any guide, the phenomenon of mother tongue transfers was there from the very beginning, as the passage from Antera Duke's diary attests. Ability to write English must have been considered from the beginning more important than the ability to speak the language.

The coming of the missionaries in the middle of the nineteenth century did nothing to alter this situation. The pressing need for the missionaries was to translate the Bible and other religious literature into the indigenous languages, hence the need to produce as rapidly as possible indigenous helpers who were *literate* in English. Sermons, from the beginning, must have been preached in the local languages - through the help of interpreters, to begin with, but soon by indigenous priests. Parish business must similarly have been carried out largely in the indigenous languages, but again, all records were kept in English. It is, indeed, significant that right from the beginning, the establishment of schools went hand in hand with proselytization. There is no reason to suppose that the missionaries had intended the English language to be propagated so widely that it became the medium of worship and of other parish activities. Even the Church of England, represented by the Church Missionary Society, did not borrow a leaf from the Church of Rome by making the English language the medium of worship. Rather, the missionaries chose to reach their congregations through their indigenous languages. The English-speaking elite produced by the nascent educational institutions were to serve as the go-between. It was they who interacted in English with the missionaries and, of course, helped in keeping the records in English.

By the turn of the century, the structures of a colonial government were in the process of being established in the country. Again, what the civil service needed urgently were the skills of literacy rather than of oracy, the civil service being a record-keeping organization *par excellence*. What is more, a good deal of even important in-house communication in the civil service takes place in writing by the procedure of minuting. The gobbledegook of the civil service soon became a familiar register of English in Nigeria.

The educational system, as we have seen, has done little to redress the balance in favour of oracy. Rather, the popular notion has been that one goes to school to learn how to read and write the English language at the primary level and then to apply these skills at the secondary and tertiary levels.

It is hardly surprising, therefore, that over several decades, the system has produced in many cases individuals with an impeccable ability to communicate in written English and be understood, even admired, internationally, without a matching ability in spoken English. It is, indeed, a fact often remarked that the general level of written English in Nigeria is much higher than that of spoken

English, and some people have even asked if there is anything wrong with this, seeing that the skills of literacy are more in demand than those of oracy.

However, it is not easy to compare achievements in the two skills. It is possible, of course, to acquire one independent of the other in a foreign language situation. In a second language situation, however, both skills are necessary, but then the danger is that they may interfere with each other. In Nigeria, for obvious reasons, the features more appropriate to written English are generally transferred to spoken English. Besides, spoken English is more susceptible to mother tongue transfers than written English. In addition to syntactic and lexical interference, to which both are subject, there is also the possibility of phonological interference in spoken English. This means that it is easier to achieve international intelligibility in writing than in speech. In addition, most Nigerians have greater access to international standards in books than in the spoken form, and this means that models of written English are more readily available than those of spoken English[3].

Indeed, barring a number of Americanisms in spelling, written English is largely standardized internationally, whereas phonologically, spoken English has several standards, and this has encouraged a desire for the standardization of spoken English in Nigeria as elsewhere. It is precisely because a Nigerian can more easily make himself internationally understood in written English than in spoken English that the standards are said to be higher in the former than in the latter. But of course, there is additionally the fact that written English lends itself to the kind of automaticity in the use of the language in the written mode than in the spoken one.

This leads us to a consideration of the question:what? What are the characteristics of the use of English in Nigeria? This has been the subject of increasing research in the last few decades. Historically, linguists' attempts to answer the question have been influenced by changing trends in the discipline. The first is error analysis, (cf Tomori, 1967). Deviations in the use of English from British norms were regarded as errors which the user must be encouraged to eliminate, and some quantification of such errors was made. But such an attitude, while perhaps inevitable at the time, would be more appropriate for a user of English as a foreign language than as a second language. Later, in order to facilitate the elimination of these errors, contrastive analyses were undertaken(cf Banjo, 1969, Afolayan, 1968). These analyses helped to establish two broad facts. One was that a bilingual learner's mother tongue does 'interfere' with his learning of a target language. The other was that certain learning errors were, in fact, universal. This may be because they relate to the universal properties of languages rather than the idiosyncratic ones, or else to universal strategies of language learning. The theories of approximative systems and interlanguage are relevant to this. Briefly, they claim that there is a natural tendency for the bilingual learner of a language to over-generalize on the basis of the limited data available to him. Further contact with more data, however, reveals the inadequacy of his approximative system which is then refined to accommodate the new data. This process of refinement goes on until the learner arrives at the optimal grammar which may or may not be identical with that at the disposal of the native speaker. The theorists of interlanguage seem more committed to the view, than those of approximative systems, that what the learner ends up with is not - and perhaps cannot be - identical with the optimal grammar operated by the native speaker.

However, it soon became clear that it was inappropriate to adopt the same attitude to all non-mother tongue users of English, if a clear distinction was to be made between the user as a second language and one as a foreign language. Standards of correctness thus became an issue. While any mother tongue English community could legitimately provide a standard for the learners of English as a foreign language (depending on the purpose of their learning the language), the immediate standard, for the learner as a second language, must be provided immediately from within the learning community itself. In other words, while all deviations in the former may legitimately be regarded as errors, some deviations in the latter must be regarded as part of the local norms. Varieties differentiation, rather than error analysis, is thus indicated for the second language situation[4].

The varieties of a langauge may be diatypic or diatopic (cf Enkvist et all, 1964). Diatypic varieties are varieties according to use, while diatopic varieties are varieties according to the provenance of the speaker. Thus within every diatopic variety are, in turn, a number of diatypic varieties relating to the various domains of use of the language. The point being made, then, was that British English and the use of English in Nigeria could be expected to be two separate diatopic varieties of the language. Of course, while it was fairly easy to describe the British variety, that of Nigeria was as yet nascent and, consequently, to a certain degree controversial. The source of the controversy was the necessity to make, in such a fluid situation, a distinction between acceptable variants and genuine errors.

Scholars in Nigeria were by no means unanimous in their view of the developing situation. There were some (e.g. Salami, 1968)who, sceptical of all attempts to set up a local standard, insisted that the British standard should continue to be used and all variations regarded as errors. The unstated fear was that an inferior kind of English might develop in the country, one which, whatever its local acceptability, might ultimately turn out to be internationally unintelligible. Others, on the other hand (e.g. Walsh,1967), argued that given the position of English as a second language in Nigeria, with all the sociological implications of that position, there was really nothing anyone could do to stop the evolution of a local standard of correctness. Perhaps we should again recall the image of the motor car. Whatever may be done to the idea of the motor car by manufacturers in different parts of the world, there are certain features which define a motor car, without which the product is, in fact, not a motor car. There are certain aspects of the grammar of English, as spoken internationally, which any diatopic variety interferes with at its own peril, and the fears of the pessimists were, it was argued, likely to turn out to be unjustified.

This is because the syntax of English is, by and large, intact in Nigeria, and syntactic deviations are regarded as errors. Local variants are to be found in idiomatic expressions - such as the famous 'He is not on seat' - lexical items, which must necessarily reflect the customs as well as the flora and fauna of the environment and, of course, aspects of the phonology. Deviations on this scale (with the possible exception of the phonological ones, which are discussed further below) are unlikely to impair intelligibility as long as the syntax remains intact.

In examining the nature of the use of English in Nigeria, it would be useful to continue to maintain the distinction between written

English and spoken English. Many of the features of written English in Nigeria are, of course, to be found in spoken English as well - including, for that matter, those which should not be - but spoken English has its own peculiarities relating to phonological features.

The first attempt at varieties differentiation in the use of English in Nigeria was made by Brosnahan (1958). Brosnahan, arguing that the varieties are educationally determined, posits four varieties. Variety I represents the performance, according to him, of those who have picked up the language outside the school system. Variety II represents the performance of Nigerians with primary eduction, Variety III those with secondary education and Variety IV those with university education. Banjo (1971; 1993) however points out that this analysis is somewhat too simplistic and therefore attempts instead a classification based on grammatical features and degrees of approximation to a world standard as typified by standard British English and RP. He also proposes four varieties in which educational attainment does play a part but is not the only determinant.

Banjo's Variety I is quite distinct from Brosnahan's Variety I, which is, in fact, Pidgin and not English. Banjo's Variety I, on the other hand, is described as the variety used by Nigerians who have picked up the language as a result of the exigencies of their occupation. Much of it can be described as 'broken English' though it should be clearly distinguished from Pidgin. Not surprisingly, the most striking feature of this variety is the phonology. For example, none of the three major Nigerian languages (Hausa, Igbo and Yoruba) has up to ten pure vowels, and only Hausa has a diphthong. RP, on the other hand, has twenty-two vowels, made up of 12 pure vowels, eight diphthongs and two triphthongs. Variety I speakers spread their much more restricted vowel systems over the more expanded one of RP, with the result that vowel contrasts are obliterated and in many cases, RP diphthongs are monophthongized. Thus:

Variety I /li:v/ is equivalent to RP /li:v/ and /li v/ (leave and live).

Variety I /kɔ:t/ is equivalent to RP /kɔ:t/, /kɔ t/ /kə:t/ and /kʌt/ (court, cot, curt and cut).

Variety I /hom/ represents RP /həum/ (home).

Variety I /faja/ represents RP /faiə/ (fire).

Furthermore, as most Nigerian languages do not have the vowels /æ/, /ə/ and /ʌ/, for example, /a/ is substituted for /ə/ while, in a word like *butter* (/bʌtə/), /ɔ/ is substituted for /ʌ/ and /a/ for /ə/. British RP /ə:/ is replaced sometimes by /ɔ:/ as in /wɔ:st/ for RP /wə:st/ (worst) or /e/ as in /fest/ for RP /fə:st/ (first)[5].

There are, similarly, substitutions of the consonant phonemes, and these vary from language to language. While some languages (like Hausa and Igbo) do have the phoneme /z/, others like Yoruba do not have it and so a Yoruba Variety I speaker would substitute /s/. Similarly,, for the speakers of some languages (again, including Yoruba) /f/ is substituted for /v/ and /ʃ/ for /tʃ/. The breaking up of consonant clusters is general.

Perhaps the treatment of the RP features of stress and intonation is even more prominent in the speech of Variety I speakers than the segmental phonemes; and again, this varies according to the speaker's mother tongue. The Kwa languages of the south are syllabic in rhythm, and this feature generally replaces the iscochronicity of stress in English. Hausa speakers, as earlier remarked, are not as prone to this transfer. Also absent from Variety I speech is the deployment of stress for emphasis. At best, a grammatical device may be substituted, so that instead of:

    I did it.

we may have:

    I was the one who did it.

More often, however, emphasis is not indicated in any overt manner.

Intonation is limited to two patterns - rising and falling - in Variety I speech. The falling intonation is used in statements, and the rising in questions and incomplete statements. The attitudinal use of intonation is completely absent.

Other prosodic features also mark Variety I speech. For Igbo Variety I speakers, the vowel harmony system is transferred to English, resulting, for example, in /fɔləu/ being rendered as /folo/, while with Edo speakers, it is the feature of nasalization which is transferred, resulting in /wen/ (when) being rendered as /wēn/. Variety I speakers of other provenance similarly transfer features from their languages.

The cumulative effect of these phonological transfers is that a native speaker of English, especially one recently arrived in Nigeria, may be present where Variety I English is being spoken and yet be totally unaware that the language is English.

As is to be expected, Variety I speech is full of syntactic transfers from the mother tongue. These include the absence or peculiar use of tense, e.g.:

*I buy it yesterday,

the peculiar use of aspect instead of tense:

*I have seen it yesterday,

frequent lack of concord:

*The books on the table is mine,

generalization of the number system:

baggages, advices, equipments,

omission of the determiner:

*I want to see doctor.

There is also the peculiar use of prepositions.

The vocabulary of Variety I is highly restricted and is likely, in any case, to be confined to the one register for which the language is needed. Outside this register, the speaker is obliged to fall back on periphrastic expressions or the use of generic terms (e.g. 'I have not got the paper' may mean ' I have not got the *letter*), or 'I have not got the *bill*', or 'I have not got the *receipt*' or even 'I have not got the *license*').

Variety II speech exhibits signs of a systematic learning of English, and its speakers are likely to have had at least primary education. Others may have had some secondary education as well and it represents the speech of most Nigerian bilingual speakers of English. The features described for Variety I are also to be found in this variety though in less density. The syntactic deviations are fewer and less gross. For example, the determiner is not likely to be omitted in the example quoted earlier, though omission of the determiner may persist in idiomatic expressions (*The football fans went *on rampage*). Tense and concord peculiarities also still persist but are less gross. The vocabulary is more extensive than that found in Variety I.

There are more phonemic contrasts in the speech of Variety II than in that of Variety I. But it is still possible, at least to a careful ear, to tell the speaker's provenance. Indeed, transfers in this variety are more phonetic than phonemic, though phonemic transfers are by no means absent.

Variety III is the product of an even greater exposure to a standard variety of the language and represents the acrolectal use of English in Nigeria. In most cases, that exposure is obtained through eduction, but it may be misleading to measure this in terms of years alone. Some speakers do not achieve Variety III until they have completed university education; others have achieved it well before completing their secondary education. Home background and quality of education at the primary and secondary levels are also important factors. At this stage, the speaker's provenance in Nigeria is more difficult to determine. Syntactic 'errors' have been largely eliminated and the speaker is able successfully to avoid areas of the grammar where he feels insecure (e.g. phrasal verbs and adverbial particles, where the more latinate expressions are preferred, resulting in a stilted style). Vocabulary is generally the forte of the speaker of this variety, though such a vocabulary has been built up more from reading than from listening. Also here, some at least of the deviations from other varieties of standard English are deliberate, representing an attempt to bend the language to the needs of a relatively new environment. Kujore (1985) and Jowitt(1991) have collected several examples which fall under this category.

As already indicated, it is not always easy to determine the provenance in Nigeria of a speaker of this variety. The phonology, though RP-based, is however not RP. As noted elsewhere (Banjo, (1971)), it shares the same deep structure with RP but has Nigerian phonetic features. Sometimes these phonetic features, though not impeding intelligibility, are strong enough to mark the speaker's provenance.

Variety IV was included in Banjo (1971) simply for completeness. It was meant to draw attention to the existence of 'Afro-Saxons' for whom English is the first language, many of whom spent the first few years of their lives in countries where English is the mother tongue, and for all of whom English continues to be the language of the home. Such individuals are admittedly very few in relation to the entire English-speaking Nigerian population. They are distinguished from the rest by the fact that they speak with the regional accent of English from a country where the language is the mother tongue, and when they eventually lose this, replace it with the standard variety of that same country. Many of them, in the course of time, may merge with Variety III.

It has rightly been observed (e.g. by Jowitt, 1991) that the identification of any particular number of varieties - or social dialects - of English spoken by Nigerians (or of any other language, for that matter) is, in the final analysis, arbitrary. There can, in truth, never be any firm dividing lines. While, for example, there is no difficulty in distinguishing between Variety I and Variety III, it is arguable that Variety II can be further sub-divided after a very close study of the data. As Jowitt has remarked, in reference to Brosnahan's (1958) classification, the new structure of Nigerian education, with a break between Junior Secondary and Senior Secondary, might provide a basis for such further sub-classification. But this would be pressing the educational parameter too far unless it can be proved to covary completely with linguistic features. On the other hand, as suggested elsewhere (Banjo, 1979) it may well be the case that generally speaking, Nigerian speakers of English attain a plateau of performance after, say, eight years of formal learning of the language. This would then account for the relatively large number of Variety II speakers. Variety III could then be accounted for in terms of greater or richer exposure, a superior facility for language learning, or a greater effort, induced perhaps by professional interests. At any rate, it is better to begin with a gross classification while the data are further examined than to set up a highly refined classification that the data would hardly support.

Bamgbose (1982) questions the inclusion of Variety IV and reduces the number of varieties to three. It is true that Variety IV speakers represent a category which is radically different from the others. While the speakers of the other varieties learn the language chiefly through the school system, Variety IV do not; whereas the speakers of the other varieties learn the language in Nigeria, Variety IV speakers generally learn it abroad and are, at least initially, monolingual speakers of the language. The Nigerian status of the variety may thus be called to question. Yet to leave the speakers of this variety out altogether is either deliberately to ignore some of the data, however small, or to deny altogether that the speakers are Nigerians. The only other alternative would be to merge them with those of Variety III, thus making that variety a little less homogeneous, though, it may be argued, not much less so than Variety II.

At any rate, the heuristic value of the present variety differentiation cannot be denied. On its basis, data can be examined and the analysis refined. But the purpose of such an exercise needs to be kept clear. The preoccupation may be with error analysis, in which the desire is to remove all deviations against the background of an agreed standard, or it may be, more neutrally, with textual analysis aimed simply at an exhaustive description of the data.

Error analysis must necessarily go on, for as long as the English language is taught in school. But, as already indicated, such errors have to be identified against an agreed standard, and that is where the other objective comes in.

It must be made clear that the debates over the choice of a standard are ultimately linguistic. They are not merely subjective or political, and it is important to examine the implications of the arguments on both sides.

The proponents of an endonormative standard draw attention to the implications of the use of English as a second language in Nigeria and to the fact that the language must necessarily adapt itself to the Nigerian environment. Therefore, the concern of Nigerians should be with ensuring that the language plays its role effectively within the country, and since the choice of an exonormative standard may militate against this, the choice should be an endonormative one. Indeed, Adetugbo (1979) goes so far as to ask:

'Should we not worry first about acceptability, especially of the spoken medium, within our immediate language environment before we set the too high a goal of international acceptability?'

These comments go to the root of the purpose of learning the English language in Nigeria. It is not learnt as a mother tongue. If it was, we should, indeed, not worry whether or not anybody outside Nigeria understands a Nigerian when he speaks English. After all, nobody is worried whether the Hausa, Yoruba or Igbo spoken in Nigeria is understood outside the country (and neither are the Americans unduly worried about the international intelligibility of their standard variety of English). Secondly, English is not learnt in Nigeria primarily as a lingua franca. If it was, we should, again, not be bothered about international intelligibility.

However, the point is worth noting that Adetugbo uses the term, *not* international *intelligibility*, but international *acceptability*. It would, indeed, be very surprising if anyone were seriously to advocate international acceptability as a feature of the Nigerian standard. The two criteria advocated by Banjo(1971) are social acceptability (which is an internal criterion) and international intelligibility (which is an external criterion). The idea of international acceptability is, indeed, one which deserves to be rejected, but not that of international intelligibility.

One of the most important features of the English language, as we have seen, is that it is today the most important international language, and this should be one of the reasons why it should continue to be learnt - whether as a second or foreign language - in Nigeria. Rather than cultivating English as a lingua franca, many Nigerians would prefer to see one or more of the indigenous languages playing that role while English, at least for the time being, continued to be the official language. If ultimately English ceases to be even the official language, it will almost certainly become an important foreign language, and then its surrender value would be judged almost exclusively by the degree of its international intelligibility.

The argument for an exonormative standard, on the other hand, errs on the other side. It amounts to treating English as if it were a foreign language in Nigeria and flies in the face of reality. It means putting the language in a strait jacket in Nigeria, preventing its adapting to, and being enriched by, the unique Nigerian environment, for every deviation from the exonormative model would be regarded as an error, or at least sub-standard. It is unlikely that such a situation would have produced any serious literature in the language in the country.

The concern by the school in support of such a model is undoubtedly for maximum international intelligibility, and its error lies in assuming that this could not be ensured with an endonormative standard. Ultimately, international intelligibility is nourished and sustained by international interaction. This is what keeps the standards in Britain, the U.S.A. and Australia mutually intelligible in spite of the vast geographical separations. The imposition of an exonormative standard would, in fact, be an artificial way of ensuring international intelligibility. As the Nigerian English-speaking community is not likely to be cut off from other English-speaking communities of the world, an endonormative standard would be well placed to ensure the international currency of standard Nigerian English.

If it is agreed that the standard should be endonormative, the next question is which of the varieties earlier described is the most deserving candidate, and the choice should be fairly obvious. Varieties I and IV can be ruled out immediately, leaving Varieties II and III. In deciding between these two, it would be useful, as earlier proposed (Banjo 1971; 1993)[7], to apply the criteria of social acceptability and international intelligibility.

The criterion of social acceptability demands that the variety to be adopted commands enough prestige in the country. If the matter were to be resolved democratically by being put to the vote, Variety II would obviously win the day since it is the variety spoken by the majority. But its prestige is not as high as that of Variety III which, unlike Variety IV, is a variety that many speakers of Variety II themselves would like to attain. Social acceptability is a crucial requirement for an endonormative standard for without it, the propagation of the variety would be difficult if not in fact impossible.

Such a basis of choice also breeds a sense of national pride in the speakers and learners.

International intelligibility is, at the same time, important for the country to maintain its membership of the English-speaking world. Otherwise, English would have to be learnt twice: first to be able to communicate internally, and then a second time to be able to do so internationally. This would be a very wasteful procedure, for whereas an internally intelligible variety need not be intelligible internationally, there is no reason why an internationally intelligible variety should not, at the same time, be intelligible internally. Obviously, on this criterion, Variety III comes off better than Variety II. On balance, therefore, Variety III would ensure a standard which is both highly socially acceptable and at the same time maximally internationally intelligible.

It should further be borne in mind that the adoption of a particular standard does not imply rigidity. Within that variety, there would, in turn, be diatypic and even diatopic varieties. It would be possible, within the variety, to speak formally, informally or intimately. Indeed, Variety III speakers of English in Nigeria today constitute a bridge between the majority of English-speaking Nigerians, who operate Variety II, and other English-speaking communities outside the country, being well at ease in either company. At the same time, the speakers of this same variety may adopt certain features of the other two varieties (i.e. I and II) as markers of degrees of informality.

At the same time, regional varieties are not likely to be completely eliminated - there is, in fact, no reason why they should be. Thus it is not inconceivable - as indeed is already the case - that there will be regional accents of the standard variety, however subtle the differences may be. It is important always to bear in mind what a large and linguistically complex country Nigeria is. With four hundred indigenous languages co-existing with English, it is hardly possible, nor is it desirable, to eliminate every trace of regional accent in standard Nigerian spoken English. Nor should the task of standardization itself be underestimated. The complexity is relieved only by the fact that there are genetic relationships among the languages.

This is seen reflected in the usages of Varieties I and II. Two entries from Jowitt(1991) will illustrate the point. First, for the verb *hear* (p.190):

'Hear.Often used as a variant of "understand"...This extension seems due to MT transfer since there is a systematic tendency in MTs for the same word to be used for *hear* (="perceive with the ear") and understand (= "grasp the meaning of)..."Hear" is also extended, particularly by V1 and V2 speakers, to mean "perceive" in general, so that the collocation "hear the smell of" is widespread.'

Jowitt's observations are accurate, and there are several other instances in which the uniformity of deviations is a reflection of typological similarities among the numerous indigenous languages. The other example from Jowitt is the verb *borrow* (p.161):

> 'Borrow.A well-known PNE(V1,V2) extension is the use of "borrow" to cover the meaning of SE "lend," e.g. "I want you to borrow me N5." It can be accounted for in terms of MT models...'

Such examples, indeed, create problems for standardization. They are so widespread that some may feel that they should be accepted as standard Nigerian usage. But this only raises the problem, also correctly observed by Jowitt, relating to the ambiguous use of the epithet *standard*. Such usages as those noted above may be regarded as being standard in the sense of being settled and even predictable (considering the size of Variety II speakers of Nigerian English), but are not standard in another sense because they do not represent the usage of Variety III speakers. Confusion may arise from mixing the technical and the non-technical senses of this word. The fact is that while it is true that some usages which are standard in the non-technical sense do also become standard in the technical sense (e.g. *He is not on seat*), many others are, at least for the time being, regarded as errors. For example, the common expression:

> 'All guests should be on their seats by 9 o'clock,'

does not enjoy the same degree of acceptance as ' He is not on seat.' While the idiomatic status of the latter is signalled by the absence of a determiner before *seat* , the former constitutes a breach of an

idiomatic use of the preposition *in*. The substitution of *on* may make the expression more natural for many Nigerian users, but it may, to a speaker of standard English, convey the unintended message that the guests are to stand on their seats.
A similar contrast is:

Lying on bed Vs Lying in bed.

One may argue that the two expressions reflect two different modes of sleeping, except that the standard English expression is regularly used to refer to both modes. If the Nigerian expression had been more literal than idiomatic, by the insertion of the determiner to give 'lying on the bed' it would be acceptable, although it would not have, for the SE speakers, and presumably for the Variety III Nigerian English speaker, the same denotation as either of the two earlier expressions.

Thus we come to the most controversial issue of all: How do we determine what is acceptable as standard Nigerian English, and who is to take the decision? We have suggested above that Variety III represents the standard, but the difficulty is that no complete grammar of this variety is as yet available. When it is, it will be the basis of teaching the language in schools as well as serving as a guide generally.

It is possible to speculate in very general terms about what such a grammar might look like. It would differ hardly at all from standard English in its syntactic component. In the phonological component, it would be marked by a Nigerian accent, or more correctly, a Nigerian range of accents. The deep phonological structure would be the same as that of standard English, but the phonetic realizations would differ from RP, Standard American or any other standard.

Next to the phonological component, it is in the semantic component, and particularly in the vocabulary, that the Nigerian standard would be distinctive from other standards. Fortunately, this area is already enjoying the attention of scholars. However, there is, as yet, no authoritative dictionary[8], and so, while scholars are agreed as to what are deviations, there is no unanimity as to which of these deviations are to be treated as errors, and which ones not. Deciding not to prejudge the issue, Jowitt(1991) describes all the deviations noted by him as characteristics of Popular Nigerian English. They feature in all varieties though obviously not to the same extent. If some of the deviations constitute common core features for all varieties while others are indexical markers, the task then is to define more closely what these common core features are. It would be reasonable to assume that standard usage would then consist of the addition of these common core features and the indexical markers of Variety III.

If Standard Nigerian English is identified with Variety III, the residual problem is how to identify these Variety III speakers in advance of the description of the variety. The definition thus becomes circular, but the only way out is to start by identifying the speakers of Variety III. The initial judgment has to be impressionistic. But speakers so impressionistically selected must then be put through the two tests of social acceptability and international intelligibility. This procedure has, in fact been used to varying extents in Ph.D. theses by Tiffen (1974), Jibril (1982) and Ekong (1985), but there is still a need for a nationally coordinated study. There are also technical matters to be settled, such as what should be the cut-off point for social acceptability and international intelligibility, once the performances of the subjects have been quantified and given a numerical value.

If the definition of a standard Nigerian English is as yet problematic, that of a standard Nigerian written English is not as difficult. Graphology does not present the same kind of problem as phonology, and certain writers - scholars and creative writers - have *prima facie* passed the twin tests of social acceptability and international intelligibility. However, Adesanoye, in a Ph.D. thesis (1973) undertook a study of Nigerian written English, and concludes by positing three varieties which, as we would expect in this case, correlate more closely with educational attainments. Thus Variety I represents, in the main, the usage of those with only primary education, Variety 2 that of those with secondary education and Variety 3 that of university graduates. This correlation is to be expected in the case of written English more than that of spoken English because literacy is typically acquired in school and normally covaries with levels of education to a much greater extent than oracy. Besides, as should be obvious by now, it is easier to measure degrees of literacy in Nigerians than those of oracy. In a non-trivial sense, all terminal examinations - from the First Leaving Certificate at the end of primary education to the degree examinations at the university level - are tests of literacy. At no level, on the other hand, has Oral English so far been mandatorily tested.

There is, not surprisingly, no straightforward correlation between Adesanoye's three varieties of written English and the varieties of spoken English earlier considered. Adesanoye's Variety 1 is roughly equivalent to the Variety II of spoken English, which constitutes a wider band in that it also includes the products of secondary education who are classified as Variety 2 writers by Adesanoye. Even some Variety 3 writers may be Variety II speakers. Spoken Variety I has no equivalent in the written varieties, and this is not surprising since Variety I speakers have no formal education. Similarly, written Variety 3 does not correspond exactly to spoken Variety III. Variety III speakers are more likely to be Variety 3 writers than the other way round. The relationship may be represented by the following schema:

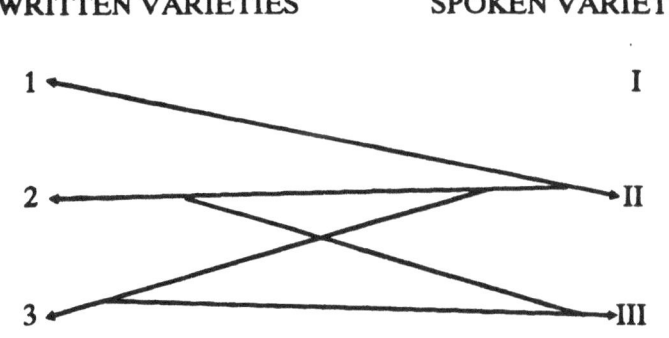

Leaving spoken Variety IV aside for the moment, and with some qualifications to be made later, this schema signifies the following:

1. All Nigerians literate in English speak either Variety II or Variety III;
2. Variety 1 writers speak only Variety II;
3. Variety 2 writers may speak Variety II or III;
4. Variety 3 writers may also speak Variety II or III.

Where the arrow points in both directions, no full reciprocity is claimed. For example, as previously remarked, Written Variety 3 writers also speak Variety II. One may speculate that if spoken English had been examined at every level as written English is, a greater correspondence between the two classifications might have been possible.

It will be noticed that the schema does not relate Spoken Variety III to Written Variety I at all. This is because although there may well be Variety 1 writers (i.e. essentially products of the primary school) who speak Variety III, this would be true mainly of the phonology of their performance. It would be less true of the syntax and even less so of the semantics. Spoken Variety IV is left out of consideration for the reasons earlier given. The written varieties correspond with educational attainments, and Spoken Variety IV cannot be said to be the product of the Nigerian educational system. In theory, though, it is not impossible to have Variety IV speakers who write Variety 2, or even I, depending on their level of education.

We may assume that there are some determinants which are common to both variety differentiations. These would be syntactic and lexical features since the spoken varieties take these into consideration in addition to phonological features. What the schema suggests, therefore, is that the syntactic and lexical features which define Variety II speakers are also to be found in the writings of all three varieties of writers. Similarly, these same features in written Varieties 2 and 3 are to be found in the speech of Variety III speakers. These are empirical matters, and what we have provided here is a hypothesis to be tested out.

The relationship of all this to the previous discussion is obvious. We are now in a position to define the speakers of Nigerian English more closely. The educational basis for the classification of the written varieties enables us in turn to use educational criteria for identifying prima facie Variety III speakers. While not claiming that all Varieties 2 and 3 writers are automatically speakers of Variety III, it would be reasonable to look among these two varieties of writers for Variety III speakers, and therefore for the standard variety of Nigerian English. The search may, purely for convenience, be narrowed down to Variety 3 writers who, after all, set the fashion, if not the standard, for written English.

Most previous researchers in the area have, in fact, intuitively assumed a convergence between Variety 3 writers and Variety III speakers. This may be heuristically harmless provided further steps are taken through social acceptability and international intelligibility tests to validate the claim in individual cases. In an attempt to define standard Nigerian English, therefore, the researcher would do well to turn to the class of Nigerian graduates, particularly those with degrees in the humanities. He may then further narrow down the field by impressionistically choosing those on whom the tests are to be administered.

The question may be asked as to how the panel of judges for the two tests are to be composed. Obviously, the data recorded from subjects will have to be subjected to two separate tests. For the test of social acceptability, the jury will have to consist of Varieties II and III speakers, with Variety II speakers in the majority, since they represent the group from which the majority of Nigerian teachers are drawn. Using the conversion now established, we know that they are products of secondary schools, teacher-training colleges or universities. It would, indeed, be wise to have teachers from the primary and secondary levels well represented in view of their strategic role in the propagation of any variety. Any speaker who is found acceptable by at least seventy per cent of the jury may be taken to have passed the test.

For the international intelligibility test, the jury would have to be composed of Variety III speakers and the speakers of other national standards, particularly standard British (perhaps not necessarily limited to RP speakers), and standard American. The choice of Variety III Nigerian participants may be made in either of two ways. If the two tests are conducted simultaneously, the selection will have to be impressionistic though, in view of what has been said so far, there are enough guidelines to ensure a reliable selection. Alternatively, if the two tests are staggered, participants may be selected from among those who have passed the social acceptability test. This, however, would mean that two different sets of data are used in the tests to avoid any single individual serving as subject and judge.

Still other important considerations have to be borne in mind. Given not only the linguistic but also the political complexity of Nigeria, careful attention has to be given to the selection both of subjects and of judges. It is, of course, a practical impossibility to have all four hundred Nigerian languages represented among the judges. Recourse would therefore have to be had mainly to the three major languages, though it may be wise now to enlarge the number to twelve. At any rate, care must be taken not to skew the selection in favour of any language or group of languages.

There are other ways in which the design of the test of social acceptability is inherently more complex than that of international intelligibility. It may be argued that at least three factors enter into the social acceptability test. The first is intelligibility, and this is basic. Unless the judges can understand what the subjects are saying, they are likely to reject them out of hand as being unacceptable. The second is the degree to which the judges identify with the data provided by each subject - i.e. whether the subject sounds Nigerian or foreign. The third factor, which in certain cases may be difficult to distinguish from the second, is the subject's voice quality. This, of course, is the least important factor but is nevertheless one which may critically colour the listener's judgment.

Tests of social acceptability and international intelligibility have by no means been standardized, but examples are to be found in Tiffen (1974), Jibril (1982) and Ekong(1985). For reliability and validity, what is required is a nationally coordinated research in which as many languages as possible are represented in the choice of subjects.

It is clear from what has been said so far why it is desirable to identify and codify a standard Nigerian variety of English, and why that variety should become the model for teaching and other purposes. It is, however, equally important to point out one function that such standardization is not meant to perform. It is not intended to fix the language once and for all in Nigeria and legislate for ever on matters of correctness. To begin with, in the absence of any authority like the French Academy, there will always be grey areas, as indeed there are in older standards such as the British. In other words, there will be cases - a very small number of them, one would hope - in which what is acceptable to one bona fide speaker of Nigerian standard will be unacceptable to another. Time can be expected to resolve the matter in many cases.

Secondly, since the standard is not expected to be a closed shop but rather a cluster of diatypic varieties, it will accommodate, in the informal register for example, slang, which is transient in nature, such usages first entering the spoken variety before, if ever, entering the written one.

Thirdly, and following immediately on what has just been said, the Nigerian standard will encourage creativity. Just as some items will pass on to the written variety from the spoken one, so others will enter the standard in the written mode and then pass on to the spoken one. Among others, Nigerian creative writers of English expression may be expected to dictate the fashion in this regard.

It therefore follows that the standard variety will have to be periodically updated. Fortunately, such updating will apply in the main to idioms and vocabulary. As is the practice with other standards, a dictionary of standard Nigerian English will be updated from time to time. This may raise a problem for English lexicography generally as there is already an attempt by the major dictionary-makers of English to reflect regional variants or peculiarities. Thus the new Collins English Dictionary, first published in 1979, with a second edition in 1986, and reprinted no less than five times since then, has fifteen consultants representing twelve national varieties of English (excluding, curiously, the American), records 'on seat' as 'West African informal' and glosses it appropriately. However, the dictionary assumes a homogeneous West African variety of English. This is not unreasonable in view of the standardizing influence of the West African Examinations Council, but as Sey (1973) and Jowitt(1991) show, there are national peculiarities within that regional variety. The question is whether Nigerian usage can be adequately covered in such international dictionaries, or a separate national dictionary should be published in addition. The latter would seem more appropriate in view of the difficulty of a comprehensive coverage in the former.

One other issue emerges from this discussion. Internationally, there is the tendency to speak more in terms of West African English than of the national varieties. West African English, in turn, is capable of two interpretations. It could mean the aggregation of all the national varieties present in the region, in which case it would not be necessary to supplement West African usage with the individual national usages; or it could refer only to what all the national usages in the sub-region have in common - usage which is current throughout English-speaking West Africa - in which case these common core features would have to be supplemented with the indexical markers from the various countries.

Similar questions have been raised with regard to the term 'Nigerian English' and 'standard Nigerian English.' Nigerian English can, in one sense, be interpreted inclusively as the totality of varieties of English spoken and written by Nigerians. It would be represented by the sum total of Varieties I to IV spoken and Varieties 1 to 3 written. It would thus be made up in part of transient learning errors - particularly common errors - and acceptable Nigerianisms. On the other hand, the term can refer exclusively to the standard variety - i.e. the written English of Nigerian graduates and the spoken English of some graduates and school certificate holders. By this definition, a distinction is made between Nigerian English, which at all times serves as the basis of acceptability in Nigeria, and any other variety (excluding IV) which is regarded as exhibiting errors of imperfect learning. In the one sense, *Nigerian* indicates no more than the provenance; in the other, it carries the stamp of social acceptability. The term tends to be used in the literature in both senses and is sometimes at the root of the disagreement between the proponents of an exonormative standard and those of an endonormative one.

If we equate Nigerian English with standard Nigerian English, new ontological problems arise. In view of the fact that there are some four hundred indigenous languages in Nigeria, how does (standard) Nigerian English differ from the standard Hausa English, standard Igbo English and standard Yoruba English? Some scholars have, in fact pointed out that it would be more practical to speak of the standards based on individual languages in Nigeria than of a national standard. This is true in the sense that if each of these language-based standards is, by definition, internationally intelligible, then all of them should, in turn, be mutually intelligible. There are, however, three possible drawbacks.

One is that while it would be easy to promote standards based on the bigger languages - and particularly the three major languages - it would be more difficult to do the same for the smaller languages, and this may produce undesirable political consequences. Secondly, since many of Nigeria's languages are genetically related, it would be better to standardize on as high a scale as possible. Various error analyses in fact reveal the similarities of mother tongue transfers in English usage in the country. Finally, and perhaps also most important, planning on a national scale is politically the most desirable. Having a standard which has been evolved nationally is preferable, for purposes of national integration, to what might end up as a large number of competing standards. It would also be preferable for teacher mobility across the country. So, while it is inevitable to have regional accents, it would be advisable to give scope to these within a national standard (9).

NOTES

1. 'New Englishes' is also the title of an anthology of essays edited by J.B. Pride (1982).

2. Paikeday(1985) had earlier proclaimed the death of the native speaker. Paikeday arrives at this conclusion by a brilliant, if not totally convincing, process of *reductio ad absurdum*.

3. This, however, is not to ignore the growing importance of international broadcasting in sound and video. These developments are bound to produce a long-term effect and will serve as a means of keeping standard Nigerian spoken English internationally intelligible.

4. This does not amount to adopting a *laisser-faire* attitude in a second language situation. Within the L2 varieties, there will be norms, and

any departures from the norms of the standard variety will be treated as errors.

5. See Jibril (1986). Jibril adopts a different system of classification. His classification is along the vertical as well as the horizontal axes. He makes a distinction between Southern and Hausa English, as well as between the basic and sophisticated varieties within the diatopic varieties. He discusses some of the differences in the phonological (segmental) systems of the speech of Hausa, Igbo and Yoruba speakers of English.

6. For some Nigerianisms in the lexis of the varieties of English in Nigeria, see Kujore (1985) and Jowitt (1991).

7. See also Banjo (1993) for an updated argument.

8. A project on a Dictionary of West African English was embarked on several years ago and reported on by the editors (Banjo & Young, 1982).

9. As previously noted, however, Jibril's study would seem to indicate a convergence between the basic varieties of the North and South. The sophisticated varieties may even be expected to converge more closely, leaving relatively trivial phonetic differences.

3

Aspects of Nigerian Bilingualism

The Nigerian bilingual deploys the two (and sometimes more) languages in his repertoire in a characteristic manner. Attention will be limited here to such deployment with regard to English and the mother tongue.

We have seen in the previous chapter the domains which compel the Nigerian bilingual to use either English or his mother tongue. Within that generalization of specialization, however, individual performances do vary, and these variations are determined in part by the individual's degree of bilingualism. The ideal bilingual is the coordinate bilingual, sometimes also referred to as the ambilingual. This ideal is more typically achieved by individuals who start off with two languages as mother tongue, although it can be argued that even this is an approximation to the ideal rather than the ideal itself. If a child grows up speaking two languages because its parents do no speak a common language, it is likely that the child will learn to specialize at a very early age in the use of the two languages at its command. Depending also on which language gets the greater reinforcement from the environment, one of the languages may quickly assume the position of dominance.

Such approximations to the ideal are much rarer in a second language situation, and part of the difficulty is that it is the second language, rather than the mother tongue, that is sociologically dominant. The coordinate bilingual in a second language situation can be defined as one who uses either language efficiently in the situations in which the use of the language is called for. It is not, by any means, one who is able to switch at will in any given situation from one language to the other. Even simultaneous interpreters do tend to specialize in the direction of interpreting and seldom regard themselves as being equally competent in interpreting in both directions[1].

Variety III speakers of Nigerian English are sometimes held up as typifying coordinate bilingualism, usually on the basis of their proficiency in the English language alone. However, it should be understood that few of them would perform to an acceptable standard in their mother tongue in the official and public domains and in the register of science and technology if they were to operate in their mother tongue. A Nigerian Variety III speaker of English may be able to write the language like a mother tongue user of the language and even speak the language nearly like a native speaker, but only in certain specific domains. His ability to use his mother tongue is also limited to certain domains, but ability to perform in either language is not vitiated by interference from the other language.

The inability of Varieties I and II speakers of English to operate the grammar of English without interference from that of the mother tongue entitles them to be defined as incipient bilinguals. Some of them may eventually evolve into coordinate bilinguals, but others may not. As we shall see later, interference is not in only one direction, for in certain situations, English does also interfere with the bilingual's mother tongue.

It is thus possible to set up a scale of bilingualism ranging from the most incipient to the most coordinate, taking into consideration both oral and written communicative competence. But first, it is necessary to examine some other features of bilingualism.

Code-switching is a common feature of the Nigerian bilingual's linguistic behaviour. Jespersen (1946) proposes a theory of energetics which, he says, explains every speaker's attempt to use the minimum possible effort in every communication situation. This would account, in a monolingual speech event, for widespread evidence of ellipsis. We may extend the theory to say that in a bilingual situation, it results in the interlocutors switching from one language to the other in the same communication encounter so as to ensure minimum effort. Exclamations and expletives in one language, for example, may be inserted in the text of the other language, e.g.

[1]Okay. Óyák'á lo. (Yoruba)
(Okay. Let's go).
[2]Good gracious! Ó ti bàjé. (Yoruba)
Good gracious! It's gone bad.

But code-switching can also be more elaborate. Sometimes the motivation is obvious, as when, for example, two Nigerians carrying on a conversation in Hausa suddenly switch to English to accommodate an Igbo or Yoruba colleague who suddenly joins them. As soon as the colleague leaves, the conversation may revert to Hausa. We may describe this as sociologically motivated code-switching. Code-switching of this category can also be used as a means of excluding, rather than of including, an intruder.

In the examples given above, however, no such overt motivation is present. A speaker who is used to the exclamations in English effortlessly inserts them into the text of another language and may find it difficult or impossible to replace them with appropriate exclamations in the language of conversation. Sometimes, however, the process is in the other direction, as illustrated by the following examples:

[3] Wallahi! I'm fed up.   (Hausa expletive)

[4] Chineke! It's broken.   (Igbo expletive)

[5] Yéè! I'm tired.   (Yoruba exclamation)

We may describe all of [1] to [5] above appropriately as examples of psychologically motivated code-switching.

In longer texts, several sentences of one language may be followed by several sentences of another, the switches varying with the shift of field and tenor of discourse. Mode of discourse is also important in the sense that code-switching occurs more frequently in speech than in writing. But it does occur in writing, frequently taking the form of proverbs, and sometimes used for stylistic effect rather than simply to obey the law of energetics (writing, being typically more deliberate, in any case calls for greater effort than speaking).

In effect, the diatypic varieties according to field and tenor which are expounded in one language for a monolingual speaker of a language are frequently expounded in two languages for the bilingual. We have seen that English in Nigeria is the language of science while the tenor between two friends engaging in an informal discussion calls for the informality of the mother tongue which they share, those parts of their discussion which are scientific (for example, dealing with processes) do call for the use of English. And so the conversation may shunt back and forth between the two languages.

The influence of the field of discourse on code-switching is usually emphasized. But the influence of tenor is also important, if more subtle. When two bilinguals who share the same mother tongue choose to communicate with each other in English rather than in their mother tongue, the reason, it is true, may be the technical nature of the subject-matter. But it may also be due to uncertainties regarding their relative status in relation to age and position. In such a situation, English is the neutral language, but also signals a certain degree of formality. The Yoruba regard for seniority, for example, is reflected in the pronominal system of the language. The plural personal pronoun is used in reference to seniors (whether by virtue of age or of position) while the singular is used for peers and inferiors. In order to avoid making a wrong choice of pronouns and causing an embarrassment, therefore, two Yoruba bilinguals may opt for English. Indeed, there is the occasional interference in this respect from Yoruba in the English of Varieties I and II speakers, and a Yoruba boy was once reported to have said to a visitor who had called to see the boy's father at home:

[6] They are sleeping,
instead of 'He is sleeping.'

Sometimes, though, two bilinguals sharing the same mother tongue (or any indigenous Nigerian language for that matter) may not agree on a choice of language, and this happens most often when they are not of equal status. Let us imagine an office setting, in which, say, a Yoruba very junior worker walks into the office of his boss, who is also Yoruba. Both of them are bilingual in Yoruba and English. The junior worker may start speaking in Yoruba to establish solidarity with his boss and in the hope of establishing personal rapport. The boss, on the other hand, may decide to deal with him purely at the official level for any number of reasons and therefore speaks to him in English. The conversation may go on in this way for some time, the boss speaking English and the junior worker Yoruba until the latter gets the message and switches to English. What he had hoped would be an informal personal encounter had turned out to be a purely official one.

But of course, the converse may also be the case. The junior worker, intimidated by his boss's high office, may choose to address him in English. The boss, on the other hand, wishing to put him at ease and appear friendly, may choose to speak in Yoruba instead. The junior worker then gladly makes a switch. Here again, change of tenor is signalled by a change of language where for monolingual speakers it would have been signalled by a change of diatypic variety of the same language. In the case of Yoruba bilinguals, it is also significant that it is the person considered to be of higher status who decides what language will be used.

Sometimes the switch is between English and Pidgin, particularly when the interlocutors in a dialogue have three languages in common - English, Pidgin and mother tongue. Pidgin, in that case, would signal familiarity while English signals formality.

A very interesting situation is one in which the interlocutors in a dialogue have three languages in common - English, Pidgin and mother tongue. It would be enlightening to study the determinants of code-switching in such a situation, but it would appear to be the case that in such instances, field of discourse and tenor each becomes a three-point rather than a crude two-point scale. On the one hand, Pidgin allows a technical discussion to take place without recourse to the mother tongue, being, as it were, intermediate between English and mother tongue. But while it is true that a good deal of technical discussion can take place in Pidgin, the interlocutors may still be constrained to shift occasionally to English (when the discussion is at its most technical) and to mother tongue (when the discussion is at its most informal). In a non-technical discussion, it would be good to know why sometimes the switch is from English to Pidgin and at other times from English to mother tongue. Part of the answer must be that Pidgin is widely regarded as the language of humour *par excellence.*

All of this is relevant to the observation very often made that even Variety III speakers do have problems operating the informal varieties of English. The fact is that for most Nigerian bilinguals, the mother tongue takes over from English in informal diatypic situations while for many, the medium is shared between Pidgin and mother tongue. Some people have therefore gone on to ask whether there is any need to teach the informal varieties of English at all within the educational system. The answer to this is that it is true that we cannot expect English as a second language to perform exactly the same functions as English as mother tongue. But at the same time, it is necessary, even in a second language situation, to make a distinction between written English (particularly at its most technical and formal) and spoken English (particularly at its most spontaneous and informal). Even though we have just spoken of a crude two-point scale of tenor, it is important to remember that this can be refined into at least a five-point scale - frozen, formal, informal, consultative and intimate. Of these five points on the scale, we would expect second-language speakers to operate confidently three - namely, formal, informal and consultative. Many of them will never need the frozen variety, while their mother tongue may be expected to replace the intimate variety. But there can be no rigid boundaries. Thus Pidgin can signify the consultative and intimate points while English and mother tongue may converge at the informal point, all depending on the other diatypic variables of field and mode.

In actual fact, there is something of a vicious circle involved. Because not enough attention is paid to spoken English in schools in the first place, Nigerian bilinguals fall back on their mother tongue or Pidgin when informal or consultative varieties are called for. Where this is not possible, they operate a formal variety of English instead - a feature that has marred even some attempts at creative writing. At the same time, because these other languages are available, it is considered unnecessary to teach the informal registers. Greater attention to spoken English will undoubtedly increase Nigerian bilinguals' ability to operate the informal varieties of English, both in speech and in writing, without rendering redundant the other languages in the bilingual's repertoire.

Code-switching should, however, be distinguished from language-mixing. Whereas the domain of code-switching is the text above the sentence unit, that of language-mixing is the sentence. Each sentence in code-switching is entirely made up of one language or another, but a sentence of language-mixing is made up of elements of two (or more) languages. Unlike code-switching which may be sociologically or psychologically motivated, language-mixing is always psychologically motivated and subject to Jespersen's law of energetics.

But first, a distinction should be made between language-mixing and lexical borrowing, which is another important feature of a bilingual's speech habit (2). The motivation for lexical borrowing from English to an indigenous language is obvious enough. Colonization had brought in its wake the importation of new articles of trade and new concepts for which there were no ready equivalents in the local languages. Two main strategies are usually employed to deal with the situation. One is calquing, as in the following Yoruba examples:

[7] asòròmgábèsì
that- which- speaks- but- receives- no- response
(radio)

[8] móhùnmáworán
capture- sound-capture- pictures
(television)

[9] ilé-ìwé
the-house-of-books
(school)

[10] ilé-ìjósìn
house-of-worship
(church).

The other strategy is borrowing. But again, a distinction has to be made between assimilated loan-words which are to be found in the speech of even the monolingual speakers of the various indigenous languages, and unassimilated loan words which are features of bilingual speech. The assimilated loan-words are made to conform to the phonological system of the recipient language whereas the unassimilated loan-words retain their English phonological shape. Bilinguals use both assimilated and unassimilated loan-words. They may even use both the assimilated and unassimilated forms of the same word. For example, the English words *teacher* and *minister* have the assimilated forms 'tísà' and 'mínísítà' respectively in Yoruba, and a Yoruba bilingual speaking to a monolingual of the language may use these forms. But in speaking with another bilingual, he would certainly use the unassimilated forms. While the presence of assimilated loan-words in the speech of a Nigerian, whether monolingual or bilingual, does not result in language-mixing, the presence of unassimilated loan-words in the speech of a bilingual is evidence of language-mixing because of the co-existence of two phonemic systems. Notice that in *tísà* /ti: a/ the affricate in the second syllable of the English source word has been replaced with a fricative since Yoruba does not have the affricate in its phonemic system. Similarly, the final schwa of the English word has been replaced with an open central vowel. In *minister*, the consonant cluster of the third syllable has been simplified with the insertion of a close front vowel in the Yoruba loan equivalent.

Sometimes, wih regard to the same item, both strategies are employed. Thus for *radio* both asòròmágbèsì and rédíò are possible, the latter, in fact, having virtually replaced the former. Similarly, for *ilé-ìwé* there is the alternative *sùkúù* (school) and for *ilé-ìjósìn, sóòsì* /   / has become a preferred alternative. The general trend, in fact, appears to favour assimilated loan-words in preference to calquing in Yoruba, and the same is true of practically all the other Nigerian languages.

Language-mixing is, however, not confined to the lexical level. Rather, as demonstrated elsewhere (Banjo,1983), it is pervasive without being arbitrary. Also, it is worth noting that language-mixing is more prevalent in the indigenous language speech of bilinguals than in their English speech. Here, the most important determinant is field of discourse, but the fact has to be admitted that many bilinguals have a wider vocabulary in English than in any indigenous language. Of the three major languages, Hausa is perhaps the least prone to language mixing with English, and this is partly because, before colonization, the language had had its vocabulary enriched through contact with Arabic, and partly because even for many decades after colonization, the language was allowed to perform much wider functions for its speakers. Even at the lexical level, the langauge tends to rely more on assimilated English loan-words than perhaps the other two major languages.

Language-mixing may at first sight appear quite arbitrary, but an examination of its syntax reveals that like any other language behaviour, it is subject to strict rules. Here are some Yoruba examples:

A. An English noun phrase may occur within a Yoruba sentence:

[11] i. All the rooms l'ó ti ready.
All the rooms it-is it perf. ready.
(All the rooms are ready).

ii. Ó ti ra five boxes.
He/she perf. buy five boxes
(He/she has bought five boxes).
Note also the borrowing of the predicative adjective in [i].

B. The lexical verb may also be borrowed but is always subject to the rules of the Yoruba verbal system:

[12] i. Wón ti paint ilé yen.
They perf. paint that house
(They have painted that house/That house has been painted).

ii Wón mpaint ilé yen l'owo.
They cont. paint house that at the moment

(They are in the process of painting that house/That house is in the process of being painted).

iii. Won a paint ile yen ni ola
They mod. paint house that prep. tomorrow
(They will paint that house tomorrow/That house will be painted tomorrow).

iv. Won paint ile yen ni àná
They paint house that prep. yesterday
(They painted that house yesterday/That house was painted yesterday).

It will be observed that in [12] i - iv above, the lexical verb is borrowed but without the verbal auxiliary, which in each case remains Yoruba. In (i), the perfective marker is ti, and the following verb is not inflected as it would have been in an English sentence. In (ii), the continuous aspect marker is the Yoruba homorganic nasal *m*, and the following verb, though English, is not inflected. In (iii) the lexical English verb *paint* is preceded by the Yoruba modal *a* indicating futurity, while in (iv), the verb *paint* is not inflected for past tense, though we know it must be past tense in view of the adverbial *ni ana* (yesterday) (3).

These examples indicate that whereas the Yoruba language does feel the need to borrow lexical items from the English language, it does not at the same time feel the need to borrow grammatical systems from the language. To put it another way, we know that all these are sentences of Yoruba precisely because the syntax is Yoruba. Thus we have:

v. Man yen
   Man that
   (That man)
but never

vi. *That okùnrin.

C. Adverbials can also be borrowed:

[13] Ó dìde slowly.

He/She stood-up slowly
(He/She stood up slo
wly).

That these are Yoruba sentences subject entirely to the rules of Yoruba syntax is also shown by the fact that they can be put through Yoruba transformational rules. Thus we can have:

[14] Mi ò like pípáìnt tí wón páint ilé yen
I neg. like nom-paint which they paint house that
(I don't like their painting that house),

where the English verb *paint* is reduplicated (*pípáint*) exactly as a Yoruba verb would have been.

D. In one isolated instance, however, the inflectional suffix may be borrowed along with an English lexical item, and that is with plural nouns. The plural of [12]v above is:

[15] Àwon men yen
pl. men demonstr.
(Those men).

Yoruba nouns are not marked morphologically for number but by means of the pronominal plural marker *awon/eyin*. What we have in [15] above, therefore, is a true mixture of two syntactic systems (4). The plurality is marked according to Yoruba syntax by *awon* and then in English syntax by the phonetic modification of *man*. It is not a simple matter of concord, however, because the demonstrative pronoun *yen* remains unaffected. So, there is an important difference between assimilated and unassimilated English loan-words in Yoruba syntax. Consider the following further examples:

[16] i. àwon sóòsi wa
pl. church our
(Our churches)

ii. àwon churches wa
pl. churches our
(Our churches)

iii. Àwon churches méfà
pl. churches six
(Six churches)

iv. Àwon sóòsi mefa
pl. church six
(Six churches).

In [16]i and ív, the assimilated loan word *sóòsì* is not morphologically marked for plurality, but *churches* is in (ii) and (iii). As we have seen, no such distinction is made with respect to the form-class of the verb.

Since it is the syntax rather than the lexis which determines the language status of a sentence, it follows that, as long as the Yoruba syntactic rules are held inviolate, practically any number of English items can occur within a Yoruba sentence. Here are two extreme examples:

[17] Ó ti run round the swimming pool six times.
He/She perf. run round the swimming pool six times
(He/She has run round the swimming pool six times).

[18] Ó run round the swimming pool six times.
He/She run round the swimming pool six times
(He/She ran round the swimming pool six times.

In [17], all the elements of the sentence but two, and in [18] all the elements but one, are English, yet to a Yoruba bilingual, each of them is a sentence of Yoruba. What we have in each case is a wholesale borrowing of an English predicate phrase into a Yoruba sentence. This gives further confirmation to our earlier observation that with unassimilated borrowing (which is strictly a feature of bilingual speech), grammatical categories may sometimes be borrowed along with lexical items. But even so, the system of the verb in Yoruba is imposed on all borrowings.

In [17], the subject pronoun ó is Yoruba. But in spite of the fact that the predicate phrase is English, the Yoruba auxiliary Aspect is substituted for the English Tense+Aspect. The rest of the predicate phrase is then left intact.

The underlying structure of [18] is similar. The subject pronoun is Yoruba, and the predicate phrase is English. But again, in the auxiliary, the English Tense(Modal)(Aspect) is replaced with the Yoruba (Modal)(Aspect). Thus, although the tense is *past*, there is no morphological marking on the verb *run*.

Indeed, the situation becomes even more extreme when we substitute a proper noun for the Subject pronoun. If we were to substitute *John*, we would have:

[19] John run round the swimming pool six times.
(John ran round the swimming pool six times).

In this case, the question may be asked: how do we know that this is a Yoruba sentence rather than a deviant sentence of English? The clues will be there in the actual *speech event* to indicate that this is an instance of language mixing rather than of code-switching. Perhaps the most overt clue would be phonological. In Yoruba, the Subject noun phrase is linked to the predicate phrase by an additional high tone realized on the final vowel of the noun phrase. Thus the sentence:

[20] Ayo sáré lo.
Ayo run go
(Ayo ran off).

is realized phonologically as:

[21] Ayoó sare lo.

where the additional syllable ó is the realization of a subject noun phrase pronominalization. Thus [21] can be glossed more literally as: *Ayo he ran off*.

Now, sentence [19], as a Yoruba sentence, would have to be said with an additional rising tone on *John*, thus making it a disyllabic word rather than the monosyllabic word that it is in English. The presence of this very basic Yoruba rule is enough, taken together with the non-marking of the verb for number or tense, to signal to the hearer that it is a sentence of Yoruba. Apart from this, a sentence like [19] can be expected to be uttered by all classes of Yoruba bilinguals, including those who cannot be expected to produce a grossly deviant sentence of English.

We may now examine what variants of [19] are also acceptable. They include the following:

[22] John sáré round the swimming pool six times.
John run round the swimming pool six times
(John ran round the swimming pool six times).

[23] John sáré yíká swimming pool six times.
John run routhe swimming pool six times
(John ran round the swimming pool six times).

[24] John sáré yíká swimming pool l'èmefà.
John run round swimming pool six times
(John ran round the swimming pool six times).

It will be observed that in [22], because the prepositional phrase *round the swimming pool* is borrowed as a block, the determiner is retained whereas in [23], the presence of the preposition yíká signals a Yoruba prepositional phrase, resulting in the absence of a determiner.

While a whole English predicate phrase may be borrowed into a Yoruba sentence, there are particular items which tend never to be borrowed in isolation and they include pronouns and the primitive prepositions *in* and *at*. Thus none of the following is acceptable:

[25] * *He* so fún mi.
He say give me
(?He told me).

[26] *Mo ti rí *her*.
I perf. see her
(?I have seen her).

[27] * Ó ngbé *in* Ibadan.
He/She cont. live in Ibadan
(?He/She lives in Ibadan).

[28] *Wón wà *at* ile.
They are at house/home
(?They are at home).

So it is generally content words rather than grammatical ones that are borrowed in isolation, and in a borrowed English noun phrase, as we have seen, (([12]v above) when the English determiner is replaced by a Yoruba one, it comes after the head word, in accordance with the Yoruba rule. The pronominal plural marker occurs before the noun, and its pragmatics is Yoruba. Thus [15] above can be compared with [29] below:

[29] Awon man yen
pl. man that
(That man).

The plural here is one of respect and the noun phrase is singular, not plural, referentially. Compare [29] with [30]:

[30] Àwon bàbá
pl. father
(Father/Fathers).

[30] is ambiguous because it can have a singular or plural reference, and an unassimilated English loan word makes it possible to avoid such ambiguity - hence also other examples like *àwon mummy/àwon mummies* (mother/mothers).

So far, we have been examining language-mixing in Yoruba sentences. It may be asked whether a similar phenomenon occurs in

English sentences. As already noted (sentences [3] to [5] above), exclamations and expletives in the indigenous languages may occur in an English text, and these are treated as instances of code-switching rather than language-mixing. An example made famous by Achebe is the Igbo rallying cry:

[31] Igbo kwenu!

interjected in an English text, and for which it would be difficult to find a suitable translation equivalent in English. Also, phatic communion may be expressed in an indigenous language in the middle of an English text, as in this example, also from Achebe (Arrow of God):

[32] Once again, Nno.

But here, we have already crossed the boundary between code-switching and language-mixing, and examples of lexical borrowing from the indigenous languages to English, though rare, are by no means absent. They are rare because in the formal situations in which bilinguals use English, English words are readily available. In any case, bilinguals tend to take a keen interest in widening their English vocabulary and generally would have to have a very strong reason for introducing lexical items from the indigenous languages. Indeed, it is the creative writers, particularly those described as the writers of the anthropological novel, who lead the way in introducing such loan words for stylistic and other effects. Such words usually describe the flora and fauna of Nigeria for which the only viable alternative may be the technical botanical and zoological terms. Examples are *iroko*,(timber) and *odan* from Yoruba. A second category of loans comes from the Nigerian culinary habits - e.g. *tuwo* (Hausa), *ogbono, egusi* (Igbo) *efo, egusi, dodo* (Yoruba). Interestingly enough, very often, instead of *akara*, the loan translation *bean cake* is sometimes used. At any rate, any item of Nigerian foodstuff or any Nigerian meal is a potential source of loan-words into the English language. Another category describes familiar aspects of communal living, hence, *bolekaja, danfo* (small passenger bus). Still another category refers to the cultural life of the people: *ozo* (an Igbo chieftaincy title), *chi* (Igbo), *egungun, ifa* (Yoruba,) and mention may also be made of the Nigerian currency - *kobo* and *naira*.

Such words as these are generally well-known across the country, but when they occur in creative writing are sometimes cushioned - hence *iroko tree, ogbono soup, ozo ceremony, ifa divination, egungun festival*. The context or co-text usually, in other cases, helps to clarify the meanings.

In speech, there is no question of adapting these items to the phonology of English. To that extent, therefore, we also have here the coexistence of two phonemic systems. However, with one notable exception which will be discussed shortly, the items are made subject to English syntax in the English sentences in which they occur. This is possible largely because the loan-words are almost exclusively nouns. Such nouns take determiners as in English (i.e. with the English determiner preceding the headword). The exception relates to the number system, which is usually indigenous rather than the English one, though instances are not unknown of the English pluralization of indigenous loan words. Thus the determiner is obligatory in [33]:

[33] A/The bolekaja   (small bus)

but the plural suffix is optional in [34]:

[34] Four bolekaja(s)

while those who are unsure opt for [35]:

[35] Four bolekaja vehicles,

thus turning the loan-word into a modifier, and at the same time cushioning it.

It is instructive to note that when the new currency system was introduced into Nigeria, the government felt compelled to announce that the plural forms of *kobo* (which had been the Yoruba word for *penny* and which had been derived from English *copper*), and *naira* (specially coined) would be *kobo* and *naira* respectively. Obviously, the intention was to stress the fact that these are Nigerian, and not English, words.

In informal speech, and particularly among young speakers, it is fashionable to borrow certain sentence-markers from the indigenous languages into English. Three such markers borrowed from Yoruba are *se, abi,* and *sa.*

[36]i. Se you are ready?
int. you are ready?
(Are you ready?)
ii. You are ready, abi?
You are ready, int.
(You are ready, aren't you?) (5)

As illustrated in [36]i and ii, *se* and *abi* are interrogative markers, and it is because of the structure underlying such sentences as [36] that Varieties I and II speakers of English do say :

[37]*You are ready, isn't it?
On the other hand, *sa* is an emphasis marker:

[38]It's broken sa
It's broken emph.
(It's indeed broken)

In [36]ii, *isn't it* is taken as a fixed equivalent of the invariant *abi.* It is interesting, though, that speakers who utter or write sentences like [37] would hardly ever utter a sentence like [36]ii, neither, generally, would the Variety III speaker who does utter [36]ii say a sentence like [37]. The explanation is that [36]ii represents conscious and creative language-mixing, whereas [37] reflects imperfect learning, assuming Variety III as standard.

Language-mixing is a phenomenon which purists in Nigeria frown upon, and this is perhaps to a certain extent understandable in view of the foregoing history of the contact between English and the Nigerian indigenous languages. There were fears at one time of English killing off the indigenous languages. But this was before the renewed interest in the study and use of these languages and the new determination to establish a balanced bilingualism. A lot of effort is at present being devoted to language treatment of the indigenous languages, and we have seen, in particular, the pilot study carried out at the University of Ife. The question now is what happens while all these efforts are being made. There are situations which typically call for the use of an indigenous language even when the field of discourse indicates English. In such a situation, the use of unassimilated loan-words would seem unavoidable, and many purists would no doubt concede this.

On the other hand, there are two other types of language-mixing which purists generally take exception to. One is what purists would describe as the indiscriminate use of unassimilated loan-words where either indigenous items or assimilated alternatives are available. The argument seems to be that, wherever possible, indigenous items should be used so that the integrity of the Nigerian indigenous language concerned is maintained. In situations where ready equivalents are not available but loan translations are, then the latter should be used. But where these, in turn, are not available, then an assimilated loan-word may be used or, if necessary, created for the occasion. It is this possibility of spontaneous coinage that makes many purists consider the use of unassimilated loan-words virtually unpardonable. What seems to be resented is not so much the fact that items are borrowed in situations where this is inevitable, but the failure to camouflage the borrowings appropriately by integrating them phonologically into the text. Loan-words, in other words, should not be allowed to stick out like a sore thumb.

The purists are, however, being unnecessarily idealistic, for the idea of a 'pure' language is simply a chimera. In spite of centuries of development, the English language itself allows a French pronunciation of *garage*, and of a phrase like *esprit de corps*, perhaps to remind us of the debt that English owes to French from the early Middle English period. The same phenomenon is observable in other languages of the world. The vocabulary of any language bears the history of cultural and linguistic contacts, and there seems to be a natural process in every case. When two languages are in contact, borrowing may be mutual, but the more dominant language must be expected to leave a more conspicuous mark on the other language than vice-versa. The process, to begin with, is spontaneous and uncontrolled, filling purists with a sense of outrage. But gradually the borrowing language re-asserts itself - as the English language did in the late fourteenth century - and the process of assimilation sets in, though this may not be total. But for every language, the process of borrowing is a continuous one, and the only language which does not borrow is a dead one.

It is, nevertheless, necessary to recognise the different official attitudes to languages, typified by Britain and France. The former allows the langauge to develop naturally, encouraging variety (6). The latter legislates on correctness in an attempt to promote a standard form of the language. Standardization is, however, a legitimate process and is subtly effected even for English by means of dictionaries, the most prestigious of which is the Oxford English Dictionary.

Countries in a hurry to develop their languages may find the French model more attractive than the English one, for the natural process may take an unconscionably long time. This is the rationale for the various metalanguage projects in Nigeria - to cut down on unnecessary proliferations and channel the efforts to develop the vocabularies of the indigenous languages. But in the end, lexicography describes rather than legislates, and its only normative role consists in often categorizing items in terms of sociolects, distinguishing between formal, informal, slang and vulgar usage.

The present day Nigerian bilingual, living under the dominance of the English language, and subject to the law of energetics, has no choice but to use unassimilated loan words freely when addressing another bilingual. But when addressing a Nigerian monolingual, he is necessarily more careful, casting about first for equivalents in the indigenous language, then for loan translations, then for assimilated loan words before, if ever, resorting to unassimilated ones. Only absolute necessity would compel him to undergo the strain of this precess. But then bilingualism is on the increase in the country, and the fear of some purists is that *Englausa, Engligbo* and *Engloruba* may consolidate themselves and successfully displace Hausa, Igbo and Yoruba respectively. However, the history of the English langauge itself does not encourage us to take this pessimistic view. Rather, the expectation is that each of the languages will emerge from the present phase sufficiently strengthened to cope with the future.

The second kind of borrowing which purists take exception to is that involving a whole predicate phrase, as illustrated in sentences [17], [18] and [19] above. As was noted, these, indeed, are extreme examples, of which sentences [22] to [24 are milder forms. And as between these three latter sentences, the purist would prefer [24] to [23], and [23] to [22]. But it must be recognized that each of these sentences ([17] to [19],as well as [22] to[24]) may have situations in which it is, if not the most appropriate, the most natural. For example, no bilingual would ever dream of uttering [17], [18] or [19] to a monolingual. By the same token, no bilingual speaking to another bilingual would think of replacing *swimming pool* in sentence [24] with a loan translation or any periphrastic expression. Of course, cultural pride may induce the bilingual speaker to eliminate altogether all these sentences but [24] from his repertoire, even if he has to be self-conscious about it. But the real task is to get him to do so without any self-consciousness whatsoever, as the most natural and most convenient way to express the meaning contained in [19]. The hope lies in a more balanced form of bilingualism preventing a situation in which the bilingual, far from engaging in a half-conscious translation from his mother tongue when he speaks English, in fact translates from English when he is speaking his mother tongue.

We have stressed so far that borrowings tend to be confined to lexical rather than syntactic categories. Intrusions into the syntactic domain are, however, not completely unknown. They may be very rare, but one example which is becoming widespread but nevertheless never fails to startle is the borrowing of the English copula construction (though never the actual English items) into Yoruba grammar. Generally, where English has a copula construction in which the copula verb is followed by an adjectival complement, Yoruba uses a predicative adjective. Thus the translation equivalent of [39] is [40]:

[39]It's red.

[10] Ó pupa
It red
(It is/was red),

while that of [41] is [42], and that of [43] is [44]:

[41] It has become red.

[42] Ó ti pupa
It perf. red
(It has/had become red).

[43] It's getting red.

[44] Ó mpupa
It cont. red
(It is/was getting red).

The above sentences indicate that there is no Yoruba equivalent of the English copula verb *be/become*. However, Yoruba does have an existential verb *wa* whose English translation equivalent is homophonous with the copula *be*. Many Yoruba bilinguals assume that the Yoruba existential verb *wa* is also the translation equivalent of the English copula. The result is the glossing of [39] as [45]:

[45] Ó wà pupa.
It exist. red,

although far more likely to occur is [46]:

[46] Ó wà red

showing clearly that the copula use of *wa* is induced by the borrowing of the adjective *red*. The choice for the bilingual at this point is between deleting the copula and using the adjective *red* as a predicative adjective on the analogy of the equivalent Yoruba construction, on the one hand and, on the other, retaining the English copula construction, in which case, in order to avoid borrowing an English grammatical item, an equivalent is looked for in Yoruba, and the Yoruba existential *wa* is pressed into service, resulting in [46], of which [45] is an extrapolation.

If the first alternative were to be chosen, we would have [47]:

[47] Ó red.

which is an acceptable piece of language-mixing, as also are [48] and [49], parallel to [42] and [44]:

[48] Ó ti red.
It perf. red.

[49] Ó nred
It cont. red.

What would be very odd is [50]:

[50] * Ó is red.
It cop. red.

or the equally odd [51]:

[51]* Ó is pupa.
It cop. red

and neither is any of the following any less odd:

[52]* It is pupa.
It cop. red.

[53]* It wà pupa

It exist. red.

[54]* It wà red.
It exist. red.

The one common source of oddness in all these sentences is the borrowing of the actual grammatical items (in this case, the pronoun and the copula) from English to Yoruba. Where the unusual need is felt to borrow a grammatical category, the need for that category to be expounded by a Yoruba item is equally felt, resulting in the extension of the existential use of *wà* to cover also the copula, as already noted.

At this stage, it may be wondered whether ultimately there may not be a semantic connection between the categories of the existential and the copula. There may well be, but whatever may be the connection, it seems clear that it is not one of equivalence.

In the phonological component, it is possible that some far-reaching changes have been set in train through the borrowing of the suprasegmental feature of stress. The trend is as yet incipient but already fairly clearly observable in disyllabic Yoruba items in which high or mid- tone is being replaced by stress, and low-tone by the lack of stress. We may illustrate first of all with the following Yoruba personal pronouns:

[55] àwa(we)

[56] èmi(I)

[57] èyin(you, pl.)

[58] àwon(they)

[59] ìwo(you, sing.)

[60] òun(he)

In all these items, the difference between the first syllable and the second, in the speech of many bilinguals, is more one of stress than of tone. Consequently, as we would expect, the vowel of the first syllable in each case is weakened and centralized and can well be transcribed as *schwa*, a vowel normally not in the inventory of Yoruba vowels. The same stress rather than tone contrasts are observable in many other words, including some of the most basic in Yoruba vocabulary:

[61] ìyá(mother)

[62]bàbá(father)

where the vowel of the first syllable is reduced except in very deliberate speech. The same stress contrast is noticeable when the contrast is between the mid tone and the high tone:

[63]apá(arm)

[64owó(hand)

[65]inú (stomach).

In contrast, where a mid tone is followed by either another mid tone, or by a low tone, the tone system is preserved:

[66]omo(child)

[67]ayò (joy)

Each vowel is fully realized in these items, thus preserving the syllabic rhythm of the language.

Obviously, this is an area deserving further study by phoneticians. What appears to be happening is that, in certain areas of Yoruba phonology, stress rhythm is acting as a counterpoint to the normal syllabic rhythm. The extent of the trend is not clear, but it is a feature of the speech of bilinguals who are familiar with both kinds of rhythm, and it operates at normal speech rate and disappears in deliberate speech.

NOTES

1. Romaine (1989) also recognizes a category of bilingualism in which there are 'poor skills in both languages' (p. 108) and describes such bilinguals as semilinguals. Many Variety I speakers of English in Nigeria would appear to fit into this category.
2. Romaine (op. cit.) makes a distinction between borrowing and 'substratum interference' (p.70).
3. It is also clear from [12]i - iv that the Yoruba equivalent of the English passive is an active one with the indeterminate third person plural subject, a feature which is often transferred to English by many Yoruba speakers of English. The same tendency is noticeable among Igbo speakers of English.
4. It is interesting to observe that in [15] the Yoruba plural marker *awon* cannot be deleted. At the same time, 'awon man yen' would be, at least, very odd if reference is to more than one man. See sentence [29].
5. There is, in fact, a semantic difference between such a sentence beginning with abi and one ending with it. Sentence [37] anticipates the answer *yes*, as suggested by the gloss. On the other hand, 'abi you are ready?' anticipates the answer *no*. This is exactly how the marker operates in Yoruba.
6. The British attitude was also extended to the former colonies, prompting Prator (1968) to deprecate the 'British heresy' of encouraging the development of endonormative standards in these second-language situations.

4

The Literary Use of English in Nigeria

When, in 1952, Faber and Faber published Amos Tutuola's *The Palm-Wine Drinkard*, the literary world was taken by storm, and certain assumptions were spontaneously made of Nigerian literature - and of African literature, of which it is part. The comments of two eminent English literary figures perhaps sum up the impressions of millions of other European readers of Tutuola's story and their preconceptions of African literature. Dylan Thomas (1952) describes the novel as

> '...a brief, thronged, grisly and bewitching story ... written in English by a West African... Nothing is too prodigious or too trivial to put down in this tall, devilish story.' (1).

and Elspeth Huxley, the well-known writer on Africa (1952):

> 'It is simply told in vivid, concise if limited English, with a flavour all its own. Mr Tutuola has had the courage and sense to go right to the roots of African art, the prerational world of spirits and magic quite unconnected with the Western frame and logic and materialism clamped down on top of it... fresh, amusing and weird... This is a book that none but an African could have imagined.' (2).

Dylan Thomas' comments are obviously more restrained than Elspeth Huxley's. While the former confines himself to the novel, though without being able to resist the urge to establish a connection between the West African provenance and the 'prodigious' and 'devilish' nature of the story, Huxley casts all caution to the winds and goes as far as telling African writers what kind of novel to write. Logic, according to her, is to be left to the Western writers while the African writer 'courageously' pursues the 'prerational world of spirits and magic' with a view to producing a work which is fittingly 'amusing and weird.' It must therefore have come as a disappointment to certain sections of the English literati that Tutuola was succeeded by Chinua Achebe and a distinguished line of other writers of fiction who, rather than displaying Tutuola's courage, have been writing about a world of real human beings not unconnected with 'the Western frame of logic' and by common consent making rather a good job of it. It seems reasonable to assume that every literature in fact has a pre-rational and magical past as well as a realistic present conveyed in a logical form, and it is surely a debatable point whether it requires more courage and sense to write one than the other. The past is as available to the Western writer as the present is to the African writer.

Huxley's prescriptivism has to do with a problem that African literature of English expression has had to contend with from the very beginning: the expectation that the literature should be unmistakably different from the metropolitan English literature. This is by no means an unreasonable expectation; what is controversial is the scope and nature of the difference.

One expects that, all other things being equal, the difference will be manifested in the use of the English language. But first, it is necessary to relate this phenomenon of creative writing in a second language to the history of the English language in Nigeria earlier discussed in this book.

The earliest contact with the English language in Nigeria dates back, as we have seen, to the sixteenth century, though the product of the contact at that stage was a pidginized form of the language. It is hardly surprising, therefore, that no literature in English was produced by Nigerians during that period. The period immediately following the end of the slave trade marked the beginning of the production of literature in English by West Africans generally. Among the authors of that era were Ottobah Cugoano, Ignatius Sancho, Phillis Wheatley and Olaudah Equiano. They were all manumitted slaves whose exact provenance in West Africa is as yet difficult to determine with certainty, although it is now generally believed that Equiano, in fact, hailed from eastern Nigeria and, apart from other evidence, attention has been drawn to the similarity between his name and the Igbo name Ekwuano. Indeed, there is a family in eastern Nigeria today who claim to belong to the same stock as Equiano. Like Cugoano, Equiano had been sold into slavery at about the age of eleven and had then worked for the next eleven years aboard slave ships sailing between the Caribbean and England. He bought his freedom at the age of twenty-one but spent many more years thereafter as a sailor before finally returning to Sierra Leone. His book, *The Interesting Narrative of the Life of Olaudah Equiano, or Gustavus Vassa the African, Written by Himself* was, we are told, an instant success.

But it must be noted that these were all writers who had gained native-like competence in the English language as a result of spending the greater part of their lives in an English-speaking environment. It may, indeed, be considered debatable, the extent to which it would be justifiable to describe them as West Africans or Nigerians. Nevertheless, it has to be admitted that each one of them learnt English as a second language rather than as their mother tongue. Their situation may, in some ways, not be too dissimilar to that of Joseph Conrad, except that they were all too conscious of their continent of origin. What they demonstrated, even before Conrad, was that it was possible to produce significant literature in a second language, and no doubt this added to the enthusiasm with which Equiano's biographical writing was received.

In the cultural history of Nigeria, the nineteenth century may be described as the century of the missionaries. In the wake of the abolition of the slave trade, missionary activity started in earnest in 1842 with the landing of the first missionaries in Badagry towards the end of that year. The missionaries at once moved inland to Abeokuta and from there established a network which eventually covered the whole of southern Nigeria.

With the coming of the missionaries, as we have seen, began the systematic and institutionalized learning of the English language in Nigeria. Although there are literary works by people of African origin elsewhere during this period - e.g. A. Crumwell and Edward Blyden - no creative writing in English came out of Nigeria. This is perhaps understandable: it was not until the turn of the century that the country became well-supplied with secondary schools, and not till 1948 that it had its first university college.

But more significantly, the prevailing assimilationist mood was hardly conducive to the use of English as a medium of creative writing. General confidence in the use of the language did not come till half-way through the twentieth century, by which time nationalism was very much in the air. The prevailing nationalistic mood brought about a questioning of the cultural influence of the colonial power, and basic to such influence was, naturally, the language. The rallying cry of the late 1940's, particularly encouraged by Indian independence in 1947, and the early 1950's was: back to the land, to the indigenous way of life; and a visual expression was given to this by the mode of dressing of the political leaders, which changed from the European to the Nigerian.

The attitude to the English language, however, necessarily had to be more complex than that to the mode of dressing. With the formal colonization of the country at the beginning of the twentieth century, English had, to be sure, become the country's official language, a status that was resented by the nationalists, whose influence on the rest of the population was particularly strong. Yet it was obvious to everyone that, in addition to being the country's official language, English had also become the language of modernization, the key to the country's desired rapid technological development. But perhaps more important was the role of English as a limited lingua franca. In this role, it made it possible even for the nationalist leaders to communicate and interact across ethnic frontiers while whatever degree of mutual intelligibility there was between the language and Pidgin enabled it to serve a more widespread important sociological function.

What some of the nationalists would have wished to see was a three-way modification of the status of English in the country. The first stage would be the replacement of English by an indigenous language as the lingua franca. The second stage would be its replacement as the official language, presumably by the same indigenous language. The third and final stage would be the restriction of the language to the tertiary level as the language of education. But unfortunately, this was an idealist programme with little hope of early implementation. The intractable problem was the choice of an indigenous language acceptable to all as a new lingua franca and official language. Discussion of an optimal language policy for the country inevitably ensued and various proposals were put forward (cf. Bamgbose (1991); Banjo, (1975),(1991)).

As was to be expected, the debate over the langauge question had its reverberations at the cultural level. Literary tradition in Nigeria before colonization had been oral and, has been pointed out by several observers (cf. Fraser (1986), among others) early attempts by Nigerians to produce literature in English were highly derivative and imitative. The question therefore arose in intellectual circles as to whether it was possible to produce African literature in a non-African language. African culture, it was argued, was so vastly different from the European culture embodied in the English language that it would be, if at all possible, at least unsatisfactory to use the language as the purveyor of Nigerian culture.

The view of culture held by such critics is one which has recently been increasingly questioned by sociologists, being one in which every culture and the language which embodies it are viewed in a water-tight compartment and completely distinct from other cultures (cf. Drummond, 1987). But even if this view was justifiable, the critics displayed considerable cynicism concerning the possibilities of cultural translation. Additionally, the water-tight compartment view of cultures is hardly borne out by reality in Nigeria, characterized as it is by 'biculturism' even more than by bilingualism.

Obi Wali (1963) was the most influential of the early critics of the use of English as the medium of African literature, and he confidently predicted 'a dead end' to Nigerian literature if it continued to be expressed in English. All that can be said about this prediction is that, thirty years after it was made, Nigerian literature of English expression, rather than displaying any signs of imminent extinction, is going from strength to strength, its authors winning various international laurels including the most prestigious of all, the Nobel Prize.

Equally influential responses to Wali were, in fact, offered by Achebe and Soyinka. In an oft-quoted remark, Achebe (1965) says:

'I feel that the English language will be able to carry the weight of my African experience. But it will have to be a new English, still in full communion with its ancestral home but altered to suit its new African surroundings.'

The current term 'New Englishes' may well owe its origin to this remark by Achebe. At any rate, Achebe here in effect affirms his belief in the possibilities of 'cultural translation' and what is even more revolutionary, simultaneously affirms the international status of the English language and serves notice of his intention to indigenize the language in Nigeria. The universalist attitude to English had become established. (3).

Soyinka's views on the subject are, predictably, similar to Achebe's. He says (Soyinka,1988):

'And when we borrow an alien language to sculpt or paint in, we must begin by coopting the entire properties in our matrix of thought and expression. We must stress such a language, stretch it, impact and compact it, fragment and reassemble it with no apology, as required to bear the burden of experiencing and of experiences, be such experiences formulated or not in the conceptual idioms of the language.'

Nothing, incidentally, better illustrates the stylistic difference between Achebe and Soyinka than the very manner in which this common credo between them is couched by each writer.

The argument over the role of the English language in Nigerian literature was but part of the larger preoccupation, in the decade after political independence, with a generally acceptable definition of African literature. There were those like Wali who believed that the medium was crucial to any such definition. Others felt that the author's provenance was no less crucial (thus asserting that African literature can only be written by Africans) while others still felt it was necessary, if not sufficient, for the subject matter and setting to be African. In the end, no neat definition could be formulated, and it was agreed that everyone could recognize the literature when confronted with it - a compromise which suffers from the inadequacies of all ostensive definitions.

At the same time, another argument had arisen, this time over who should be the audience of African literature. Some of the early writers had been accused of writing the anthropological novel because they were aiming at a non-Nigerian audience. Such writers, it was claimed, often felt obliged to explain Nigerian customs explicitly in their writings - indeed, the motivation for writing in the first place, it was claimed, was simply to explain Nigeria's 'exotic' culture to the outside world. Young (1971) illustrates this class of West African novel with this passage from Akpan's *The Wooden Gong:*

> A girl's fattening involved at least three months -in some areas it could involve as many and more years - in a secluded place under heavy, and regular enforced feeding. During this period she would do nothing whatsoever but eat, wash and sleep. Any type of food she wanted would be provided, and the more she ate the more she would please her parents and her prospective husband. To avoid her doing any form of work, many maidservants were placed at her service. As an additional means of achieving as much weight as possible a lady specializing in the trade of fattening girls would be hired for the task of regularly massaging the girl, who should lie flat with belly on the floor... The amount of weight put on at the end of the period would indicate the wealth of the girl's parents, and the efficiency of her fattening woman and of her maidservants.'

The novelist is Efik from south-eastern Nigeria, and obviously if he had thought that he was writing only for Efik bilinguals like himself, he would not have belaboured this explanation of a well-known Efik custom in the middle of a narrative. But it would be wrong, at the same time, to jump to the conclusion that the author was writing exclusively for a British or American audience. The fact is that a great majority of non-Efik Nigerians would also benefit from the explanation. Nigeria's national literature can, after all, at present be written only in English.

More skilled writers are able to be economical and less didactic by making use of an elegant cushioning device or by using the context and co-text to gloss unfamiliar terms and concepts, as Achebe does in the following passage from *No Longer at Ease* (1960):

'The President, in due course, looked at his pocket watch and announced that it was time to declare the meeting open. Everybody stood up and he said a short prayer. Then he presented three kola-nuts to the meeting. The oldest man present broke one of them, saying another kind of prayer while he did it, "He that brings kola-nuts brings life," he said. "We do not seek to hurt any man, but if any man seeks to hurt us may he break his neck." The congregation answered *Amen*. "We are strangers in this land. If good comes to it, we have our share." *Amen*. "But if bad comes let it go to the owners of the land who know what gods should be appeased." *Amen*... "An only palm-fruit does not get lost in the fire." *Amen.*

This is quintessential Achebe, an inimitable choice of English structure and lexis to convey a memorable blend of Igbo cosmology, Igbo humour and the Igbo predilection for proverbs which, as Achebe says on another occasion, are 'the palm oil with which words are eaten.'

The argument over audience, which was regarded as influencing the particular use of the English language in various ways, came to a head with the exchange between Chinweizu et al (1975) and Soyinka (1975). Chinweizu et al in effect accuse Soyinka of failure, or even refusal, to communicate with the ordinary Nigerian bilingual, and of using in his poetry esoteric language aimed at communicating with an audience outside Nigeria. Soyinka stoutly responds by defending his right to explore the whole gamut of the Nigerian condition, including the modern aspects, and to choose his imagery from the full range of the contemporary Nigerian experience.

A writer's style is obviously partly an expression of his personality as well as a reflection of the complexity of his subject matter, but it is also possible, in Nigerian literature of English expression, to make a broad distinction between medium-oriented writing and message-oriented writing, without necessarily making value judgments about the relative merits of the two. Besides, there is nothing to show that a writer like Soyinka or Okigbo is more easily accessible generally outside Nigeria than inside.

The proposed distinction between medium-oriented and message-oriented Nigerian writing is one which, obviously, has to be made with caution. No writer writes successfully without having something to say. At the same time, none writes successfully either without due attention to his medium. But in spite of this, it is possible to make a distinction between a writer like Achebe who calls attention to his use of the English language to portray the cultures- and particularly the speech-types- of Nigeria, infusing new life into the English language in the process, and Soyinka, who more readily calls attention to the working out of a philosophy of universal validity, a philosophy fashioned out of an inter-penetration of European and African thoughts. In the process, he uses the kind of language which Chinweizu et al, as we have seen, deprecate. Paradoxically, it is the density of Soyinka's language, rather than the complexity of the ideas being expressed, that tends to strike most readers more forcefully. It is not accidental that Achebe is primarily a novelist whereas Soyinka is primarily a poet.

The writing of realistic novels calls for linguistic verisimilitude, which in turn calls for linguistic differentiation of the characters. Achebe's genius lies, in part, in his ability to differentiate his characters linguistically, conveying consistently their linguistic status as monolingual Igbo speakers, bilinguals in Igbo ad English of various degrees of communicative competence, and bilinguals in Igbo and Pidgin.

In contrast, we may consider Soyinka's *The Interpreters*, a highly successful novel, but one which is quite different from the typical Achebe novel. Soyinka draws his main characters from a narrower social class and all of them are articulate bilinguals, so that linguistic differentiation among them is uncalled for and might even have distracted attention from the main preoccupation of the novel. Besides, apart from the setting of the novel, very few linguistic clues of the characters' provenance is offered (apart from those given by their names) though the presence of monolingual Yoruba speakers is acknowledged on at least one occasion. The preoccupation of the novel is with the exploration of ideas.

We would have expected that as a dramatist, Soyinka would share some of Achebe's concern for linguistic differentiation. But the conventions of drama are necessarily different from those of the novel, though it is possible to have an intersection between the two, since either can be highly realistic or highly conventional. Achebe's handling of dialogue in his novels is conventional in the sense that it would be contradictory in real life to have a monolingual Igbo speaker speaking any form of English at all. What Achebe has done is to create a variety of English to represent the speech of such a monolingual speaker, and the attempt is acceptable because it does manage to operate the thought-channels of the Igbo monolingual speaker (4). In stories that deal to any extent with the clash of cultures (or sub-cultures), such linguistic differentiation is an important ingredient of the aesthetics of a work of art. But in novels - or plays - which have other preoccupations, the linguistic differentiation of characters may be based on other criteria. Thus in *The Lion and the Jewel*, Soyinka's convention comes closer to Achebe's than in *Madmen and Specialists*. In *Death and the King's Horseman* we have a more complex play than *The Lion and the Jewel* but with similar linguistic features because the speech of Yoruba monolinguals have to be presented in English. In neither play, however, does linguistic verisimilitude appear to be a major preoccupation.

Having made this broad categorization into which all Nigerian writing can be fitted, it remains true that all Nigerian writers have to make the English language 'carry the weight of their African experience.' In very general terms, they do this through a careful selection of structures and through a legitimate manipulation of the lexico- semantic possibilities of the language.

A number of studies have been made in recent years of this subject. At the non-literary level, Adesanoye (1973) has made a study of the English prose of the various categories of judicial officers in a region of Nigeria. He is able to establish three categories covarying with the officers' educational background and professional experience. He is able to identify some common-core features in the use of English by all of his subjects, but at the same time, he discovers a progressive approximation to 'world standard' English, particularly at the syntactic level, as he moves from Variety 1 to Variety 3. The common core features amount to what Jowitt (1991) describes as the features of Popular Nigerian English.

The model for Nigerian written English has tended to be Educated British English which itself is a variety of world standard English. Adesanoye's varieties are therefore inevitably established in terms of departures from what is agreed to be educated British English. This methodology has increasingly been criticised by Kachru (1985) and by others who have been influenced by his writings. According to them, the varieties of English which have developed in the 'outer circle' (Kachru, op.cit.) should be described in their own terms and not by comparison with a standard from the 'inner circle.' Thus instead of saying, as Adesanoye would have said, that the magistrates make more 'mistakes' in their English prose than the High Court judges, what look like 'errors' have to be characterized in some other way, as Nigerianisms which are inevitable in view of the second-language status of the English language in Nigeria. The three varieties are then just regarded as three social varieties of written Nigerian English, just as there are social varieties in the inner circle itself, and one of them may be regarded as standard.

An illustrative attempt to describe the phonology of Indian English in its own terms is made by Mohanan (1992). It is, however, perhaps easier to adopt this methodology in phonological and lexical descriptions than in syntactic ones. The real problem seems to be that Nigerian English has to be accounted for in terms of either more or fewer rules than those producing standard varieties of the language elsewhere, including the inner circle. If this is so, we have to determine what the input to these rules is in the first place. It seems possible to admit that the input is a variety from the inner circle (given, particularly, the institutional context of learning the language) without necessarily making a value judgment. After all, the intention cannot be to deny that there is a historical and pedagogical connection between British English and Nigerian English. Even so there also is between British English on the one hand, and American and Australian varieties of English, on the other, and it is always possible to describe each of these in relation to another.

It is, as has been noted, precisely this feeling of the relative autonomy of the English language in Nigeria that has made it possible for internationally acclaimed literature to be produced in the language in the country.

The strategies at the disposal of the Nigerian writer of English expression are, as shown by Johnson (1981) and Osakwe (1992) by no means infinite and operate at the syntactic and lexical levels, but also at the rhetorical level.

The option at the syntactic level is basically one of selection, since the syntax of a language does not generally lend itself to the kind of inventive manipulation that the lexis does. Generally speaking, the options open to the Nigerian writer here are no different from those open to the mother tongue writer. But we may note two notable exceptions with regard to the writings of Amos Tutuola and Gabriel Okara.

Tutuola remains perhaps unique among internationally recognized Nigerian writers. Abroad, he was hailed, perhaps for the wrong reasons. He was regarded as belonging simultaneously to the categories of medium-oriented and message-oriented writers. As a medium-oriented writer, he was regarded as deliberately using the English language in a rather unique way with little regard for the standard syntax of the language or for its lexical rules. At the level of discourse, his rhetorical strategies were also found to be unusual. At home, Tutuola was immediately recognized as writing Variety 1 of Adesanoye's classification. The deviations, it was urged, were not deliberate but rather, as noted elsewhere (Banjo, 1972), Tutuola was telling Yoruba folk-tales in the only kind of English he was capable of.

This perhaps raises echoes of the intentional fallacy. Does it matter at all whether or not the deviations are deliberate? What effect should such considerations have on the appreciation of Tutuola's novel as a work of art subject only to the laws of its own being? What part, indeed, should be played by a knowledge of the sociology of the writer in the appreciation of his work? These issues are still, interestingly, live today, and Soyinka, exasperated by what he considers an obsessive preoccupation with the sociology of the creative writer, has called for attention to be shifted for a change to the sociology of the critic (Soyinka,1988).

But the fact is that both at home and abroad, critics have chosen not to ignore Tutuola's sociology. The comments by Dylan Thomas and Elspeth Huxley quoted at the beginning of this chapter show that the critics' response is not unrelated to their knowledge of the writer's nationality and, in Huxley's case, to presuppositions about African writing. Would the response have been the same if the writer had been an Englishman or an American?

This is not an easy question to answer. E.E. Cummings took great liberties with the syntax of the English language, and British critics might have seen Tutuola as an even more exotic version of Cummings. Moreover, the success of Mark Twain shows that prose fiction does not always have to be written in the standard variety of the language.

All the same, it is perhaps not easy for critics to filter out any knowledge they may have about a writer in assessing his work, in an attempt to fully contextualise that work. Nigerian critics therefore read Tutuola's novels in the context of what they know of the author's education as well as of the effect that his knowledge of Yoruba folk tales may have had on him. The problem is that, unlike Mark Twain, Tutuola is not writing in a geographically identifiable dialect of English as mother tongue; and yet, unlike E.E. Cummings, his language is not deliberately idiosyncratic. Perhaps it is inevitable that Tutuola's use of English should be differently evaluated. Another very important consideration is that, as already remarked, Nigerians have been accustomed to regarding written English as the model of English usage, and many people are therefore worried about the effect that Tutuola's English usage may have on school children in particular, and generally on all those whose chief aim in reading a novel is to improve their English proficiency.

As a message-oriented writer, Tutuola was regarded abroad as basing his first novel on the archetypal quest motif. Again, critics at home deny that this is deliberate, but rather assert that the motif was there in the first place in the Yoruba fables and so, as more or less a griot, Tutuola could not properly claim the credit for it. Again, it seems possible to look at the matter from two perspectives. First, irrespective of sources, the quest motif in the novel can be examined and critically appraised. Secondly, if one is so inclined, one can examine Tutuola's treatment of his source material - whether he has merely reproduced it or tried to adapt it in a personal way, as Soyinka has done with the Yoruba Ogun myth. Tutuola's claim to the membership of the group of message-oriented writers would, in fact, depend on the proof of any such adaptation, and the end to which it is put.

Nevertheless, we should be wary of making too much of the conscious process involved in the act of literary creation. Tutuola may well have manipulated his source material in certain ways at the subliminal level, as a medium which every literary artist is.

We may now illustrate Tutuola's style with this passage from *Feather Woman of the Jungle* (Tutuola, 1962):

> 'In the fourth night, when the people gathered in the front of my house and drinks were served as they were dancing and singing with great joy. Then I stopped them and I addressed them first as follows: "I am very happy indeed to see you again in front of me and I thank every one of you for the great affection you have on me, although I am head of the village. And I wonder greatly, too, to see that you are increased again this night more than 90 per cent. But (all sat quietly and paid great attention to me) when I first saw the whole of you I was afraid, but after I thought it over again my fear was expelled.'

At the textual level, there is the elevated tone of the whole passage, suggesting a formal translation from the author's mother tongue:"*I wonder greatly;*" "*this night;*" "*After I thought it over again my fear was expelled*". But there are many other noticeable features of the language. The first 'sentence' is incomplete, and this is purely idiosyncratic as it is not the result of a transfer from Yoruba. Many would regard it as a feature of Tutuola's interlanguage.

Then there are the odd expressions/collocations, in some cases involving an unusual use of the preposition: *In* the first night; in *the* front of my house; the great affection you have on me. Notice also the use of *the whole of you* in the last sentence where *all of you* might have been expected. Earlier on, *all of you* and *everyone of you* had, in fact, been used as expected. It is the accumulation of such features that led critics to observe a perfect match between content and language in Tutuola's first novel.

In *The Voice*, Gabriel Okara also uses the English language in a remarkable way, but this, in his own case, is a deliberate act. He himself says (Okara, 1973):

> 'As a writer who believes in the utilization of African ideas, African philosophy and African folk-lore and imagery to the fullest extent possible, I am of the opinion the only way to use them effectively is to translate them almost literally from the African language native to the writer into whatever European language he is using as his medium of expression.'

From this point of view, *The Voice* may be seen as an experimental novel. It has had a mixed reception, but it is difficult not to regard it as a failure. Okara's literal translations include expressions such as:

> 'His inside was sweeter than sweetness.' (p.71)

which, admittedly, has a poetic ring about it and might have been unobtrusive in a poetic work; but also, at the syntactic level: :

> 'through the black black night Okolo walked. (p.76)

Again, the inversion of subject and adverbial, and the repetition of *black* would attract no special attention in poetry. One is therefore tempted to conclude that here, unlike in Tutuola's novels, we are confronted with a confusion of registers in which the language appropriate to poetry is applied to prose fiction.

Such examples show Okara, who not surprisingly has written some fine poetry, as representing one extreme of medium-oriented writing in this novel, through his attempts to operate the English language through an occasional fusion of the syntax and semantics of Ijo and English in the writing of prose fiction.

More similar to Tutuola than to Okara are the authors of the Onitsha popular literature. There is no conscious manipulation of the language here, but only a desire to imitate the popular romantic novels originating from England. This literature is fascinating in its own way, with its unintended parody of the English popular romantic novel. The language of the dialogues is appropriate to the characters, who are generally drawn from the minimally educated classes of society. Although they can hardly be held up as models of the use of English, the novels do accurately reflect common attitudes and conventional wisdom, and seldom fail to amuse. Obviously, all that the authors are concerned about is telling a good story, sometimes in dramatic form, in Variety 1 English (*sensu* Adesanoye) and with maximum humour, though sometimes also with overt didacticism (5). Their particular use of English will be examined later.

Other writers of prose fiction who may be classified as medium-oriented follow, with varying degrees of success, Achebe's example in his prose fiction. On the other hand, there is a different sense in which every poet must be highly aware of his medium. The conventions of poetry make it easier for the poet than for the novelist to be inventive in the use of language, and as Johnson (1981) has demonstrated, the medium makes it possible for West African poets to draw their metaphors and imagery from the West African environment and allows for quite explicit cultural translation, including the transliteration of local lores and proverbs.

The influence of the indigenous culture and locale may be explicit, as in these three stanzas from J.P. Clark (Soyinka, 1975:314):

' He serves
The ford between swamp and sand,
He serves!

In Ojoto
So they worship the masks,

Altho' in season -

The masks!
O take off the mask! And behind?
What wind! What straw.'

lines which are evocative at once of the culture and of the flora and fauna of the Delta region of Nigeria. Clark's poetry, as has often been remarked, is particularly rich in such imagery.

In Soyinka's poetry, allusions to Yoruba mythology and an evocation of the Ifa gnomic poetry provide a cultural contextualization. This is best illustrated from his poem,*Idanre*. In *The beginning*, we have the following stanza (Soyinka,1975:53):

'Low beneath rock shields, home of the Iron one
The sun had built a fire within
Earth's heartstone.Flames in fever fits
Ran in rock fissures, and hill surfaces
Were all aglow with earth's transparency
Orisa-nla, Orunmila, Esu, Ifa were all assembled
Defeated in the quest to fraternize with man.'

But at other times, Soyinka's cultural translation operates at a deeper, more abstract level, giving rise occasionally to charges of obscurantism. The predominance and prominence of nouns in his *Animistic Spells* (Soyinka, 1975:70) is reminiscent of the naming which characterizes some genres of Yoruba poetry, even outside the well-known *oriki:*

'V

Incense
Of pines when a page
Is turned, woodsmoke
Rings
Across a thousand years to a bygone sage

VI

Fragments
We cannot hold, linger
Parings of intuition
Footsteps
Passing and re-passing the door of recognition

VII

Line
Of the withered bough
Hill and broken valleys
Dearth
On thirsty palm to furrows of the earth'

A relatively new but refreshing voice is that of Niyi Osundare. Originally a linguistic scholar, he is already making an international impact. Here is his poem *Earth* (Osundare, 1986) written in the *oriki* mode and obviously drawing inspiration from the same source as Soyinka's poem just considered:

Temporary basement
and lasting roof

first clayey coyness
and last alluvial joy

breadbasket
and compost bed

rocks and rivers
muds and mountains

silence of the twilight sea
echoes of the noonsome tide

milk of mellowing moon
fire of tropical hearth

spouse of the roving sky

virgin of a thousand offsprings
Ogeere amokoyeri

The dramatic genre, like prose fiction, offers the possibility, as we have noted, of using language for purposes of characterization, and here, as Achebe does in the novel, playwrights in varying degrees follow the example of Shakespeare (cf Clark, 1968) in using language as a convention to represent different speech-types. For the Nigerian playwright, as for the Nigerian novelist, the problem is to represent monolingual speakers of indigenous languages as speakers of English. But the range of speech-types varies from play to play. In plays such as those presented on television depicting contemporary Nigerian life, speech differentiation is made among characters of the same social class, or at best between speakers of different varieties of English. At other times, the range is wider, taking in both contemporary urban life and traditional rural life, and the success here is very uneven.

At still other times, the play, though in English, seeks to present rural life only minimally disturbed by modernity. Perhaps the best-known example of this kind is the serial, *The Village Headmaster*, presented on television. The series is seriously flawed by the handling of the language of the monolingual Yoruba characters. The result is that an important character like Chief Eleyinmi is reduced to a caricature, even a buffoon. Perhaps the best speech representation in the series is Pidgin.

Yet drama presents the widest scope for presenting a variety of speech-types, the impact all the more striking because of the oral presentation. Playwrights like Wole Soyinka, Ola Rotimi and Femi Osofisan have exploited the possibilities to suit their particular purposes. Code-switching often takes the form of songs sung in the indigenous languages. In Ola Rotimi's plays in particular, it may also take the form of asides and expletives in an indigenous language to reinforce the prevailing atmosphere (6).

To what extent do Nigerian writers set the fashion for the emerging standard Nigerian English? Here it is necessary to make a distinction between serious Nigerian literature and ephemeral Nigerian literature. An example of the latter is the Onitsha popular literature earlier referred to (7). Some of it is prose fiction and some drama, though it is not known how widely the plays have in fact been performed. The language, as earlier remarked, reflects Adesanoye's Variety 1 usage, and indeed, part of the fascination of the literature lies in the use of language which some may describe as colourful, and others as bizarre. It was once seriously debated whether in fact this can rightly be described as literature, but Obiechina (1971), drawing attention to the conscious manipulation of language by the authors, remarks (p.116):

> 'There is no doubt that the popular market pamphlets are literature; they satisfy our broadest expectations of works of literature. Their authors are keenly aware of linguistic implications; in fact, they are obsessed by the effects of language and the possibilities of language in the hands of creative artists.'

There is no doubt that this literature, aimed at the very large population of minimally educated Nigerians bilinguals, has had the effect of strongly reinforcing Variety 1 writing habits. Here, for example, are lines from a play, "Elizabeth My Lover" by Okwenwa Olisa (Obiechina, 1971):

> 'Elizabeth my daughter talk less, you are addressing your dad. My own is that you can marry Ototofioko...He cannot compel to marry this old, illiterate Chief Jaja with dirty teeth and dirty clothes. Your right must be respected.'

But the play does contain some linguistic differentiation between the variety of English noted above (and observe how the speaker, considering herself educated, looks down on the "old, illiterate (Chief Jaja)" and Pidgin, which is presumably the speech type of the illiterates like Chief Cookey, who exclaims in the same play (8):

> Elibeth! Elibeth! My parlour dirty you no washing it with broom. We tin you dey do since morning. You no following me go farm. You stay for house and you no fit do any homework. You no be better person. The day way I go beatam you, you go die that day. Government no go asking me any thing,'

Such writing, apart from being highly entertaining, also has implications for status planning, one of the features of language planning highlighted by Cooper (1989). Pidgin is here associated with the illiterate population, placed far below Variety 1 English. By reinforcing the prejudice against Pidgin, the authors ensure a continued low status for the language. By contrast, the status of Variety 1 English is enhanced.

If popularity (together, perhaps, with business success) is what the writers of the Onitsha market literature are looking for, the authors of serious literature aim at something more enduring. A purely literary study of African literature of English expression would attempt to identify themes and motifs, but it is possible also to identify the linguistic resources with which the authors' objectives are pursued.

It is remarkable, in a country in which university education is not wide-spread, that nearly all serious writers are university graduates, most of them possessing a degree in the Humanities. This fact must have an important bearing on the work of each one of them. For one thing, it determines their authorial prose (in fiction), their authorial voice (in poetry) and their deployment of speech types in drama and dialogues.

It can be safely argued that through their own personal performance, Nigerian serious writers promote Variety 3 English and the syntax and lexis of Variety III spoken English. Not only have Clark, Achebe and Soyinka each produced a school with gifted followers, the generality of Nigerian bilinguals have also been influenced by these writers. Young Nigerians are exposed to their works at the secondary and university levels and have consciously or unconsciously imbibed from them strategies for making the English language "carry the burden" of their Nigerian existence. They are learning how to temper the English language with the thought-channels of the various indigenous Nigerian languages. They are learning to adopt an imaginative attitude in particular to the semantic component of Nigerian English.

With the phonological component, however, the influence is not so strongly felt, and we may examine this by looking at the two main media of dramatic production in the country - stage productions and television productions (9).

Until the establishment of J.P. Clark's repertory company in the 1980's, serious drama production in Nigeria was confined to the university campuses, the University of Ibadan Arts Theatre, in particular, maintaining a vigorous tradition of productions. The cast is usually mostly students, but occasionally, more experienced amateurs also participate. This setting obviously has normative implications for spoken English, which in fact is assiduously cultivated, as we would expect, in the various Departments of Theatre Arts. The university students who crowd the theatres to watch the plays are exposed to attitudes to the varieties of English and come away with ideas of standards. But the students form only a small minority of the country's population, and the motivation for changing already established speech habits is never very strong. So, although they are influenced - or perhaps rather confirmed - in their attitudes to various speech types - the indigenous languages, Pidgin, the three broad varieties of Nigerian English - they may identify with Variety III without being able dramatically to adopt it in their own performance.

But an even more important point is that few characters on stage are models of Variety III, anyway, with the result that an upper band of Variety II is all too often substituted for it, and this is particularly noticeable with respect to the suprasegmental features of stress, juncture and intonation. Performance in these areas is, in fact, not much different from that of most of the audience. It is the variety most often heard among students on the campuses, bearing witness to the neglect of spoken English in the country's educational system.

A great deal of the effect of drama derives from the oral interpretation of the lines. The dramatists - Soyinka and Clark, for example - assume this in their plays, but hardly enough justice is done to it by the players.

For a more conscious promotion of Variety III spoken English, we must turn to the electronic media, to the presentation of news in the federal radio and television networks. The State electronic media houses are not as consistent, and in many cases feature Variety II. The explanation may be that at the beginning, news readers on the federal networks received adequate training. Whether that is still the case is uncertain, but a firm idea of a standard seems to have been inculcated not only in the news readers but also in those who select them. It is impossible for this Network English not to have influenced performance generally in the country, but that influence would have been much greater if all those who take part in discussions on radio and television also tended towards the same standard. Of course the Network must reflect all the varieties of English spoken in the country, but a broadcasting house must, at the same time, have its own house standards which are projected, as presumably all broadcasting houses do all over the world, in news bulletins and a number of 'high profile' programmes.

Dramatic productions on television present us with quite a different picture. There are programmes like *Masquerade,* featuring the inimitable Chief Zebrudaiah, which are the electronic equivalent of the Onitsha pamphlets earlier discussed, except that the speech of the chief defies all categorization. It is a unique blend of Variety I English, Pidgin and Igbo, while the other characters speak either recognizable Pidgin, Variety I English with generous interlarding with indigenous languages, or code-switch between that variety and the indigenous languages. As with the Onitsha market literature, much of the entertainment comes from the use of language, with the *tour de force* coming from the chief himself. But there is an important difference, namely, that linguistic entertainment in *Masquerade* is more deliberate than in the Onitsha literature.

The portrayal of characters like Chief Zebrudaiah, and Chief Eleyinmi of *The Village Headmaster,* however, raises an important point already hinted at. It does appear in both instances that their speech is meant to be a conventional way of representing indigenous languages. If this is so, it has to be admitted that the attempt in each case is a failure. Achebe has shown how an indigenous language can be represented in dignified English in the mouth of a chief or any other respected member of the community. What we have in the case of these two television serials (though more so in the case of *The Village Headmaster)* is analogous to a palace scene in which the king himself is the jester. If the portrayal in each case is deliberate rather than a failure of art, it then becomes tempting to read an ideological meaning into the serials.

At any rate, both programmes reinforce the stereotyped attitudes to the speech types presented. As the setting is rural, the only types of English presented are Varieties I and II, with the former predominating and fully exploited for comical effects. Clearly in such a setting, Variety III would be out of place, the implication being that it is the variety spoken by city-based (and in most cases highly-educated) people.

Exploring another kind of experience are the plays produced on television with great regularity but obviously on a shoe-string budget. They are often grossly under-rehearsed, and some of the characters can actually be seen on occasion reading from badly concealed scripts. The setting is usually urban and the situations modern. Here, then, is an opportunity of naturalizing the English language in Nigeria, using it to explore the English-speaking Nigerian bilingual's predicament. But unfortunately, it is largely an opportunity lost.

Nevertheless, even such plays do sometimes present realistic linguistic differentiation. The prevailing variety of English tends to be Variety II, but there are sometimes realistic instances of language-mixing and code-switching (the last being meaningful only in linguistically homogeneous States).

Then there is the soap opera broadcast on the federal television network in which the cast is made up partly of professionally trained actors and partly of fairly experienced amateurs. This is usually very narrowly-based social drama depicting the city-based Nigerian elite. The variety of English predominantly featured is Variety III, even occasionally tending towards IV. Variety II, when it occurs, is usually reserved for servants and other obviously less well-educated characters. The viewers are thus led to associate Variety III with the successful upper-class while Variety II represents the speech of the lower classes. The series obviously has normative possibilities.

This brief review leads to a number of conclusions. First, it is clear that not all creative writers and not all broadcasting stations, consciously promote a standard of English in Nigeria. But at the same time, to the extent that practically all of them feature different speech-types, their works reveal attitudes to these various speech types. All the works are in English. Yet there is a clear difference between the language of Onitsha literature and that of the serious writers already referred to in this chapter. The difference, as we have seen, is due as much to the educational background of the authors as to that of the envisaged primary audience. With particular reference to the electronic media, there is a difference between, on the one hand, the language of the newscasters and of the more sophisticated soap opera, and, on the other hand, the language of such serials as *The Village Headmaster* and *Masquerade*. The difference here reflects that between the quality of the scripts as much as of the actors. But the attitudes to the different speech-types remain the same: Variety I English for the barely educated; Variety II for the moderately educated; and Variety III for the sophisticated. It is suggested that even though the writers of the scripts may not be being tendentious, these attitudes are part of the impressions left with the viewer and may or may not appreciably influence his or her own performance.

All the works, though in English, have occasion to present the speech of monolingual speakers of the indigenous languages. This, as we have seen, they have done with varying degrees of success. In the hands of the unskilled writer, the result is a comical effect which may be unintended. Where intended, the idea is to poke fun at an 'illiterate' character (10). Where unintended, it is simply a failure of art.

Finally, it is significant that all the authors do recognize that the English language co-exists with Nigeria's indigenous languages and Pidgin. Some of them have sought to reflect this social reality in their works, again with varying degrees of success. Pidgin is generally rated by the writers as lower in status than any variety of English, but it is not always clear how Pidgin compares in status with the indigenous languages (if it is not, itself, to be regarded as one). Some writers, as we have seen, tend to lump the two together, using a speech-type which is a mixture of Pidgin and Variety I English to represent both. At the other extreme, Achebe endows the representation of an indigenous language with a dignity all its own, making it often richer than any other variety of English. Language-mixing and code-switching tend to be avoided by the writers except, to a limited degree, in drama, where it is more likely to be used for comic effect than to heighten realism.

The fact remains, however, in view of all this, that while there is evidence that some attempt is made by Nigerian writers to reflect the linguistic reality in Nigeria, it is more difficult to demonstrate to what extent the writers in turn, through their works, affect linguistic attitudes and practice in the country. That they are bound to do so, however, can hardly in the nature of things be denied.

NOTES

1.&2. These quotations are taken from the blurbs on the 1952 edition of *The palm wine Drinkard*.

3. From *Aesthetic Illusions*, Soyinka(1988:86-109).

4. This is why the reader is overwhelmed by a sense of realism in spite of the conventional use of the English language.

5. The authors are, themselves, people of humble education. Highbred Maxwell's "Our Modern Ladies Characters Towards Boys" reproduced by Obiechina (1971) has this in the author's Introduction:

'At long last Beauty repented, although it was medicine after death. She, heartbrokenly died a miserable lonely and lamentable death. She died the worst death as nobody mourned her.'

Even more interesting is this passage, also taken from the same epistolary novel:

'She started the letter with good writing and grammar full of good English.
The letter reads;
Primary School Centre
Isuochi- Okigwi
19th Oct. 1959.

My dear Young Teacher,
I sieze this opportunity to inform you that I am waiting for you an account of what you told me last week. I should not have got the chance to inform you this because we are being worried from revision but owing to the blindness of love, I manage it so.

I wish to hear from you soon
Yours truely in love
Miss Beauty Ikeofor.'

6. This is particularly striking in productions of his play, *Kurunmi*.

7. Why is the literature produced in English? The authors are surely under no illusion that they are producing a national literature. Rather, they are thinking of a readership around the bustling commercial city of Onitsha. Nor can they, because they write in English, be accused of aiming at an audience outside Nigeria. The only other possible reason is that the authors feel more at home *writing* English than Igbo.

8. This two-way differentiation is in contrast to Achebe's four-way differentiation. Achebe presents Pidgin, a variety of English representing Igbo speech and Varieties 2 and 3 of Nigerian English. Occasionally, of course, he also presents British native-speaker English, such as at the end of *Things Fall Apart*.

9. The home-grown Nigerian cinema, on the other hand, is dominated, not by English but by the indigenous languages, particularly Yoruba. A national film company has recently been established and it remains to be seen what impact this will have linguistically.

10. In Nigeria, the term *literate* tends to be narrowly interpreted, referring only to anyone who is literate *in English*. There are, of course, many Nigerians literate in, for example, Arabic and/or their own mother tongue. Such people are nevertheless referred to as illiterates. Another term similarly narrowly construed is *educated*.

5

Prospects

In view of the naturalizing processes which the English language has inevitably been undergoing as described in the previous chapters, it is reasonable to ask what the envisaged end of these processes is. There are in this connection perhaps only three options.

The first is that, having fully naturalised, the language would be on its way to becoming an indigenous language in the country, and one which, in time, might well assume the status of the mother tongue of some Nigerians. This would, in effect, put the country in the category of such countries as the United States of America, Australia, New Zealand and parts of Canada in which the language has firmly put down roots outside its ancestral home. English would, in effect, become a Nigerian language and would be a strong candidate for the status of official language and lingua franca, thus putting an end to the contest between the three major indigenous languages.

But it is very doubtful if this would turn out to be an acceptable development generally. For one thing, the debate over a national language has been going on for some time, and the general feeling is that a choice has to be made from the existing indigenous languages in the country. As long as the language goes by that name in Nigeria, English is not likely to be regarded as fully appropriated and may continue to be regarded as essentially exoglossic. Besides, before English becomes fully appropriated, the question of a national language may already have been settled.

The second option is for the country to join the category of the Scandinavian countries of Denmark, Norway and Sweden in which the English language is very widely spoken without its being the official language. Again, this would hardly be an appropriate model since it would mean changing the status of the language in the country to that of a foreign language. Such a change would hardly be possible without another language ready to fill the role of official language. In a country like India, this may be a possibility since English already shares the status of official language with Hindi. In Nigeria, it would simply create a vacuum.

This leaves us with the third option, namely, that of retaining English as a second language in the country. Hitherto, part of the definition of English as a second language in Nigeria is that it is the country's official language. But this need not necessarily be so for an indefinite period of time. Following the development in India, one could envisage a time in the future when English would share the status of official language with one of the country's indigenous languages. But many Nigerians would wish to see a later development in which the role of official language is filled by an indigenous language alone. If and when that possibility does come to pass, we would have a situation in which the country has one official language (chosen presumably from one of the existing three major languages) and two lingua francas (i.e. the official language and English). It would be interesting to watch developments in India, which has already reached the stage of two official languages and where Hindi is spoken by well over 100 million people.

In effect, the current definition of a second language as it applies to Nigeria would have to be modified to cover the widespread use of English without its being the official language. But this situation would be different from that obtaining in the Scandinavian countries earlier referred to because whereas the language remains exonormative in Scandinavia (with constant close physical contact between the countries and Britain) it will have become endonormative in Nigeria.

If it is granted that the English language will remain indefinitely Nigeria's second language, it becomes necessary to define its position more closely in relation to the country's four hundred indigenous languages, and this brings us to the consideration of an optimal national language policy for Nigeria. This is a matter on which Nigerian linguists have exercised a great deal of thought, and it would be fair to say that most of them, including the present writer, would agree with the views expressed on the matter by Ayo Bamgbose in his various writings on the subject and recently restated in a wider context in Bamgbose, 1981. These views envisage one of the existing indigenous Nigerian languages emerging as the official language while at the same time a role is carved out for English as the language of wider communication. But whereas many people would like to see the situation brought about by a government fiat, Bamgbose counsels a gradualist approach in which the policy is implemented in stages. This is in line with the views expressed above whereby English moves from its present position of the sole official language to being one of two official languages and finally to being a (second) lingua franca without being an official language.

Bamgbose's advocacy of a gradualist approach is, however, based more on the processes for the choice of an endoglossic lingua franca, an aspect of an optimal language policy which is not of great relevance to us here except in so far as it raises the important question of how many languages an educated Nigerian would be expected to have in his repertoire. The present National Policy on Language in Education (first formulated in 1977 and revised in 1981 but yet to be implemented) deals with four categories of languages: the mother tongue, the language of immediate community, the three major languages (i.e. Hausa, Igbo and Yoruba) and English.

The policy subscribes to the view that initial education is best conducted in the learner's mother tongue and therefore provides for the first three years of primary (as well as all of pre-primary) education to be conducted in the pupils' mother tongue. But appreciating the multilingual nature of the country's population, the policy also provides, in appropriate cases, for the language of the immediate community to be so used. This constitutes an admission that some Nigerian children will never receive education at any level in their mother tongue. It is not clear what percentage of Nigerian children will be so affected, but the problem is likely to be concentrated in the large urban areas as well as in some remote rural villages. In either case, the language of immediate community is certain to be one of the languages elsewhere used as medium of instruction.

The policy further provides that the medium of instruction after the first three years of primary education should be English. This, of course, follows from the provision that English should be taught as a subject from the first day of primary education.

For the secondary and tertiary levels, the policy provides for English to be the medium of instruction but makes it mandatory, at the secondary level, for one of the country's three major languages to be learnt, provided it is not the learner's mother tongue. This means that the native-speakers of any of these major languages would end up as trilinguals speaking any two of the major languages and English. Admittedly, the native speakers of these three languages constitute more than fifty per cent of the country's population, but still, it does mean that tens of millions of children who are native-speakers of the other languages may well have to be quadrilinguals speaking their own mother tongue, the language of the immediate community, one of the three major languages and English. In actual fact, the number of Nigerians to be so affected may be smaller than imagined since for many, the language of immediate community may well turn out to be one the three major languages.

Thus the products of the policy will be, in the majority of cases, trilinguals in English, one of the three major languages and another indigenous Nigerian language. Doubts have been expressed (e.g. by Christophersen, 1948:2) as to the feasibility of operating a quadrilingual, or even trilingual education, and this may eventually have a bearing on the implementation of the policy. Whatever happens, the positions of English and the three major languages are unlikely to be affected. Neither is that of the mother tongue which, unlike the other languages, is not acquired at school, anyway. The problematic category is the language of the immediate community in so far as it implies the learning of an additional language. But even that is not as unfortunate a prospect as the possibility of millions of children not being able to have initial education in their own mother tongue.

We may now focus more closely on the position of English within the policy described above. At the time that the national language policy in education was formulated, the variety of English intended to be taught in schools was, clearly, a 'world standard' based on the British standard. The first question to ask therefore is whether the evolving Nigerian English can adequately replace this standard. This question can be answered in the context of the discussion of Nigerian English earlier presented in this book. If Variety III is cultivated as the basis of standard Nigerian English, the transition can be expected to be smooth for, as we have seen, this variety, apart from being socially acceptable, is also internationally intelligible. Thus no hardship would be worked on the policy.

It is, however, necessary to examine the implications of Variety III not being chosen and consciously cultivated as the standard. The only threat to Variety III is Variety II, which is spoken by more Nigerians than Variety III. If Variety II were to get established, perhaps by default, as the standard taught within the educational system, a number of consequences are bound to follow which must have implications for the national policy. The most important implication is that in course of time, the variety may be seen as being inadequate for some of the nation's needs. It might prove inadequate for international transactions. But even more importantly, it might prove inadequate for the demands of higher education. Already, complaints are rife about the level of proficiency in English of the products of secondary education in the country. This is because Variety II, rather than Variety III, dominates teaching at the primary and secondary levels, often in spite of the standard suggested in the text books. If the situation is perpetuated, it will became necessary to institute the teaching of English for Special Purposes both for students going on to the tertiary level and for all those who need to use the language internationally.

Now, English for Special Purposes (ESP) is a phenomenon usually associated with situations in which English is a *foreign* language, and this suggests that the adoption of Variety II (and given a continuing naturalization process) may lead to English becoming a foreign language in the country, thus justifying the fears expressed by Prator (1968). Indeed, there is the long-term possibility that a Variety II-based Nigerian English may come to occupy the position of an English-based creole. This implies that English would have to be learnt twice within the educational system: the Variety II-based variety at the primary level, and an internationally intelligible (and presumably exonormative) variety at the secondary level. This would not only overload the language content of the syllabus in schools but would represent an unjustifiable waste of time and effort, for the time spent cultivating Variety II at the primary level could quite easily have been spent cultivating Variety III, thus making every Nigerian capable of using the English language for both internal and international communication. Moreover, the cultivation of Variety III would prevent a perpetuation of the present position in which English helps to stratify the Nigerian society. A relevant discussion of attitudes to the English language in Anglophone Africa is to be found in Schmied (1991).

It should be remembered that Variety III itself is not homogeneous. The important point, however, is that even the lowest bands of the variety would be at least minimally internationally intelligible. Students at the tertiary level, for example, would operate the upper bands in keeping with the professions for which they are being prepared.

Another possibility is that a situation of diglossia may arise between Varieties II and III. The main question here is whether such a situation should be planned and what benefits would accrue from such planning. Indeed, the situation is no different from that just described above, if the effect is that some Nigerians would be able to speak only the Low variety while others are able to speak both the High and the Low varieties. If, on the other hand, the intention should be that all educated Nigerians should be able to command both varieties, it is not clear what the advantage of this would be over cultivating just one variety, i.e. Variety III.

As earlier remarked, Variety III is not homogeneous. This is true not only in terms of the proficiency of those who speak it, but also in terms of the diatypic sub-varieties contained within the variety. Along the axis of mode, the variety is capable of differentiation between formal and informal, and even between slang and informal. This being the case, it would be unnecessary to give any special recognition to Variety II. A speaker of Variety III would, on appropriate occasions, be expected to move close to Variety II, and on others, to operate at the upper bands of Variety III. In fact, part of the responsibility of the schools would be to teach appropriate usage within Variety III, thus making it unnecessary formally to teach any other variety.

The advantages of adopting Variety III as the Nigerian standard, and of teaching it alone within the country's educational system, are thus clear. Meanwhile, the linguistic environment will continue to influence the English language in the country, just as the language, in turn, will continue to influence that linguistic environment. The function of a language policy is to impose well-motivated order on what would otherwise be chaos, but in doing so, due regard would have to be had for realism, and particularly within the educational system, for what is feasible, even allowing for Cooper's (1989) argument that a language policy is always pursued to serve the interests of the ruling elite. A trilingual language policy in education would appear to be the ideal option, one in which every Nigerian is proficient in his mother tongue, in one of the three major languages which is not his mother tongue and in English. But unfortunately, it would be impossible to prevent some individuals ending up with three languages in their repertoire, and others, four, because although the educational system may operate in terms of a trilingual policy, none of those three languages may,in the case of many children, be their mother tongue.

But there would be inequity even among those who do have only three languages in their repertoire. A native-speaker of any of the three major languages would end up being proficient in two of the three major languages whereas others would be in only one. Another inequity which is perhaps of greater concern to many Nigerians is the advantage to be conferred on those Nigerians whose mother tongue is eventually chosen as the national language. For this reason, many influential speakers of some of the so-called minority languages have, in fact, advocated the continuation of the *status quo*. It remains to be seen, however, what the strength of general support for this point of view is in the country. In theory, the combination of the present education policy which guarantees nine years of education for all Nigerian children, and the language policy in education which in effect ensures nine years of the learning of English, would be to make all Nigerians proficient in English. The same combination of policies would also result in every Nigerian being proficient in one of the three major languages. The hope is that the pattern of choice of major language would eventually make the selection of an official language easy, but that remains to be seen. The only language, as a result of the policies, that is sure to be spoken by everyone is English. Would this, perhaps, tilt the balance in favour of the language? It is difficult to tell. The three considerations to be reconciled are nationalism, equity and feasibility.

As just remarked, feasibility would point in the direction of English, particularly a distinctly Nigerian variety of the language which in course of time would be spread through the educational system. Equity may point in the same direction, for it means that all the indigenous languages are placed at the same disadvantage. This, of course, would not be entirely true, for there would still remain the fact that some children would not be able to receive initial education in their mother tongue unless a very complicated way is found round the problem. Even so, many may argue, the inequity would be reduced by the adoption of English as the official language. Nationalism, on the other hand, uncompromisingly demands that the official language should be one of the existing indigenous languages of Nigeria. These nationalist feelings tend to be very strong, so much so that it is assumed that, in the end, they will carry the day and necessary sacrifices will be made to minimize the resulting inequities. This, in fact, seems to be the assumption underlying the national policy on language in education.

In confronting these problems, Nigeria is no different from most of those former colonies of Britain which have had English as their official language. Like Nigeria, such countries are also trying to work out an optimal national language policy which would satisfy the demands of nationalism while preserving the many advantages of retaining English as a lingua franca. Obviously, these countries will, in the years ahead, have much to learn from one another.

All we can say for now is that the English language in Nigeria is alive and vigorous, and that the omens for its future are propitious, whatever sociolinguistic label may be considered appropriate for it in the course of time: it will, for the foreseeable future at least, be the language, internally, of higher education, of a rich and internationally acclaimed literature and of big business, and externally, of most of the country's international transactions.

Bibliography

Achebe,C. (1975)The African Writer and the English Language. *In Morning Yet on Creation Day.* London: Heinemann.

Adejare, O.(1992)*Language and Style in Soyinka: A systemic Textlinguistic Study of a Literary Idiolect.* Ibadan, Heinemann Educational Books.

Adekunle,M. (1974)The Standard Nigerian English in Sociolinguistic Perspective. *Journal of the Nigeria English Studies Association,* 6(1).

--- (1979)Non-random Variation in (the) Nigerian English. *In* Ubahakwe,E. *(ed)* op.cit.

Adeniran,A. (1979)Nigerian Elite English as a Model of Nigerian English. *In* Ubahakwe,E. (ed) op.cit.

Adetugbo,A. (1977)Nigerian English: Fact or Fiction. *Lagos Notes and Records,* 6.

--- (1979)Nigerian English and Communicative Competence. In Ubahakwe,E. (ed) op.cit.

Adesanoye, F.A. (1973)A Study of Varieties of Written English in Nigeria. Ibadan, PhD Thesis.

Afolayan,A. (1968)The Linguistic Problem of Yoruba Learners and Users of English. Ph.D. Thesis (London).

--- (1987) English as a Second Language: A Variety or a Myth? *Journal of English as a Second Language,*1.

Agheyisi,R. (1971)West African Pidgin English: Simplification and Simplicity. Ph.D. Thesis (Stanford).

BIBLIOGRAPHY

Akere,F. (1982)Sociocultural Constraints and the Emergence of a Standard Nigerian English. *In* Pride,J. (ed) op.cit.

Amayo,A. (1980)Tone in Nigerian Englis h. *Papers from the Regional Meeting of the Chicago Lingui*stic Society,16.

Bailey,R.W. & M. Gorlach (eds) (1982) *English as a World Language.* Cambridge: University Press.

Bamgbose,Ayo (1971)The English Language in Nigeri a. *In* Spencer,J. (ed) op.cit.

--- (1973)*Language and Society in Nige*ria. Stanford: University Press.

--- (1982)Standard Nigerian English: Issues of Identification. In Kachru,B. (ed). op.cit.

---- (1991)*Language and the Nation. The Language Question in Sub-Saharan Africa.* Edinburgh: University Press.

Banjo, Ayo (1967)Some Comments on the Grieve Report. *Journal of the Nigeria English Studies Association*, 1(2).

------ (1969)A Contrastive Study of Aspects of the Syntactic and Lexical Rules of English and Yoruba. Ph.D. Thesis (Ibadan).

------ (1970a)On Competence and Performance in a Second Language. *Ibadan Studies in English,* 2(1).

------ (1970b)A Historical View of the English Language in Nigeria. *Ibadan,* 28.

------- (1971)Towards a Definition of 'Standard Nigerian Spoken English.' *Actes du 8e Congres de la Societe Linguistique de l'Afrique Occidental,* Abidjan.

------(1972)Aspects of Tutuola's Use of English. *Spectrum Monograph on African Literature,* Vol 3:Georgia State University.

---- (1974)On the State of English Studies in Nigeria. *Journal of the Nigeria English Studies Assoc*iation, 6(1).

----- (1975)On Writing Revision Grammars. *New Journal of Approaches to Language* Arts,1.

------ (1979)Beyond Intelligibility. *In* Ubahakwe,E.(ed) *Varieties and Functions of English in Nigeria.* Ibadan: African Universities Press.

BIBLIOGRAPHY

Banjo, A. & P. Young (1982)On Editing A Second-language Dictionary:The Proposed Dictionary of West African *English*. *English World-Wide*, 3(1).

Banjo, Ayo (1983)Aspects of Yoruba/English Language Mixing. *Journal of Nigerian Languages*,1.

--- (1988)A Crique of the Decreolization Model of Second Language Development. *Journal of Behavioural Research*, 2(1).

---- (1991)On Language Policy Design and Implementation. *In Language Teaching In Today's World.* Paris, Hachette.

--- (1993)An Endonormative Model for the Teaching of the English Language in Nigeria. *International Journal of Applied Linguistics*, 3(2).

Bloomfield,L. (1933)*Language*. London: Allen & Unwin.

Brosnahan, L.F. (1958)English in Southern Nigeria. English Studies, 39(3).

Cassidy,F.G. & R.P. Le Page(1967) *A Dictionary of Jamaican English.* Cambridge: University Press.

Chomsky N. (1957)*Syntactic Structures*. The Hague: Mouton.

--- (1965)*Aspects of the Theory of Syntax.* The Hague: Mouton.

Christophersen,P. (1948)*Bilingualism: An Inaugural Address.* University of Ibadan.

Clark, J.P. (1968)The Legacy of Caliban. *Black Orpheus*, 2(1).

Cooper, R.L. (1989) *Language Planning and Social Change*. Cambridge: Cambridge University Press.

Davies, A. (1991)*The Native Speaker in Applied Linguistics*. Edinburgh: University Press.

Desai, G. (1993)English as an African Language. *English Today*, 9(2).

Drummond,L. (1987)Are there Cultures to Communicate Across? An Appraisal of the 'Culture' Concept from the Perspective of Anthropological

Semiotics. *In Developments in Linguistics and Semiotics : Language Teaching and Learning Across Cultures.* Washingtown: Georgetown University Press.

Dunstan, E, (1969)*Twelve Nigerian Languages.* London:Longman.

Ekong, P.A. ((1978)On Describing the Vowel System of a Standard Variety of Nigerian Spoken English. Ph.D. Thesis (Ibadan)

Elugbe, B.& A. Omamor (Forthcoming) *Nigerian Pidgin: Background and Prospects.* Ibadan: Heinemann.

Enkvist,N.,J. Spencer & M. Gregory (1964) *Linguistics and Style.* London: Oxford University Press.

Fishman, J.A. (ed) (1968)*Readings in the Sociology of Language.* The Hague: Mouton Publishers.

Foley, J. (ed) (1988)*New Englishes: The Case of Singapore.* Singapore: Singapore University Press.

Forde, D.(1956)Efik Traders of Old Calabar. London. Cited in Spencer, J. (ed) op.cit.

Fraser, R. (1986)*West African Poetry.* Cambridge: University Press.

Fyle, C. & E.D. Jones (1980)*A Krio-English Dictionary.* Oxford: University Press.

Grieve,D.G. (1966)*English Language Examining.* Lagos: West African Examinations Council.

Hallet,R. (ed) (1964)*Records of the African Association,* 1788-1831. London Cited in Spencer, J, (ed) op. cit.

Hancock, I.F. (1971)West Africa and the Atlantic Creoles. *In* Spencer,J. (ed) op.cit.

Jacobs, R. et al (1966)*English Language Teaching in Nigeria.* Lagos: Federal Ministry of Education.

Jespersen, O. (1946)*Mankind,Nation and the Individual From a Linguistic Point of View.* London: Allen & Unwin.

Jibril,M. (1982a)Phonological Variation in Nigerian English. Ph.D. Thesis (Lancaster).

---   (1982b)Nigerian English: An Introduction. *In* Pride,J. (ed) *New Englishes. Rowley*, Mass: Newbury House.

---   (1986)Sociolinguistic Variation in Nigerian English. *English World-Wide* 7.

Johnson,A.C. (1981)Language and Society in West African Literature: A stylistic Investigation into the Linguistic Resources of West African Drama in English. Ibadan, PhD Thesis.

Jowitt,D. (1991)*Nigerian English Usage:* An Introduction. Ikeja: Longman Nigeria.

Kachru,B. (1966)Indian English: A Study in Contextualization. In Bazell, C.E..J.C. Catford, M.A.K. Halliday & R.H. Robins, *In Memory of J.R.Firth*. London: Longmans.

---(ed)   (1982)*The Other Tongue: English Across Cultures*. Urbana: University of Illinois Press.

---(ed)   (1985)Standards, Codification and Linguistic Realism: The English Language in the Outer Circle. In Quirk,R.&H.Widdowson (eds) *English in the World: Teaching and Learning of Languages and Literature*. Cambridge: University Press.

Kirk-Green,A. (1971)The Influence of West African Languages on English. In Spencer, J. (ed) op.cit.

Kujore, O. (1985)*English Usage. Some Notable Nigerian Variations*. Ibadan: Evans Brothers.

Mafeni, B. (1971)Nigerian Pidgin. *In* Spencer, J. (ed) op.cit.

Mazrui,A. (1975)*The Political Sociology of the English Language. An African Perspective*. The Hague: Mouton.

Mesthrie,R. (1992) *A Lexicon of South African Indian English*. Leeds: Peepal Tree Press.

Mohanan,K.P. (1992)Describing the Phonology of Non-Native Varieties of a Language. *World Englishes*, Vol II, 2(3).

Obiechina, E. (1971) *An African Popular Literature*. Cambridge: University Press.

Obilade, A.O. (1984) On the Nativization of the English Language in Nigeria. *Anthropological Linguistics*, 26.

Odumu, A.E. (1981) Aspects of the Semantics and Syntax of "Educated Nigerian English. Ph.D. Thesis (Ahmadu Bello University, Nigeria.

----- (1984) Educated Nigerian English as a Model of Standard Nigerian English. *World Language English*, 3.

Okara, G. (1973) African Speech...English Words. In Killam, G.D. (ed) *African Writers on African Writing*. Northwestern University Press.

Omolewa, M. (1975) The English Language in Colonial Nigeria. *Journal of the Nigeria English Studies Association*, 7.

Osakwe, M. (1992) The Language of Soyinka's Poetry: A Diatype of English. Ibadan, PhD. Thesis.

Osundare, N. (1986) *The Eye of the Earth*. Ibadan, Heinemann.

Paikeday, T.M. (1985) *The Native Speaker is Dead!* Toronto & New York: Paikeday Publishing Inc

Platt, J., H. Weber & M.L. Ho (1984) *The New Englishes*. London: Routeledge & Kegan Paul.

Prator, C. (1968) The British Heresy in TESL. In Fishman, J.C.A. Ferguson & J. Das Gupta (eds), *Language Problems of Developing Nations*. New York: John Wiley & Sons.

Pride, J.B. (ed) (1982) *New Englishes*. Rowley, Newbury House.

Rens, L.L. (1953) *The Historical and Social Background of Surinam Negro English*. Amsterdam. Cited in Spencer, J. (ed) op.cit.

Romaine, S. 1989 *Bilingualism*. Oxford: Blackwell.

Salami, A. (1968) Defining a Standard Nigerian English. *Journal of the Nigeria English Studies Association*, 2(2).

Sapir, E. (1921) *Language*. New York: Harcourt, Brace & World.

Schmied, J. (1991) *English in Africa: An Introduction*. London: Longman.

Sey, K. (1973) *Ghanaian English: An Explorative Survey*. London: Macmillan.

BIBLIOGRAPHY   163

Soyinka, W. (1975)*Poems of Black Africa*. London: Heinemann.

----- (1988)*Art, Dialogue and Outrage*. Ibadan: New Horn Press.

Spencer,J. (ed) (1971)*The English Language in West Africa*. London: Longman.

Strevens,P. (1981)Forms of English: An Analysis of the Variables. In Smith, L.E. (ed) *English for Cross-Cultural Communication*. London: Macmillan.

Tiffen,B. (1974)The Intelligibility of Nigerian English. Ph.D. Thesis (London).

Tomori,S.H.O. (1967)A Study in the Syntactic Structures of the Written English of British and Nigerian Grammar School Pupils. Ph.D. Thesis (London).

Turner,L. (1949)*Africanisms in the Gullah Dialect*. Chicago.

Tutuola, A. (1962)*Feather Woman of the Jungle*. London: Faber & Faber.

Ubahakwe,E. (1974)Bookish English Among Nigerian Students. *Journal of the Nigeria English Studies Association.*, 6(1).

----- (1979) *Varieties and Functions of the English Language in Nigeria*. Lagos: African Universities Press.

Wali,O. (1973)The Dead End of African Literature. *Transition*:4(10).

Walsh,N.G. (1967)Distinguishing Types and Varieties of English in Nigeria. *Journal of the Nigeria English Studies Association*, 2.

INDEX

Abeokuta, 11, 14, 123
Achebe, Chinua, 67, 122, 125, 126, 128, 129-130, 136, 139, 141, 143, 145; *Arrow of God,* 110; *No longer at ease,* 126, 128; *Things fall apart,* 146n8
Africa, South 62; West, 3,4,11,14,62,122
Afro-Saxons, 61, 65, 79
Akpaṇ, *The Wooden gong,* 127
America, Discovery of (1492), 62
Animistic spells (Soyinka), 137
Arrow of God (Achebe), 110
Asia, 62
Association of Lecturers of English for Academic Purposes, 57
Australia, 29, 43, 62, 64,67, 82, 147

Badagry, 11, 14, 123
Baptist Academy, Lagos, 45
Bayero University, Kano, 57
Blyden, Edward, 14, 123
Bonny, 2
Britain, 11, 16, 17, 41, 44, 61, 62, 82, 114, 148
British Council, 50, 56, 57

Calabar, 2, 11, 35
Cambridge, University of, 17
Canada, 34, 62, 148
Chomsky, Noam, 39-40
C.M.S. Grammar School, Lagos, 1, 45
Church Missionary Society (C.M.S.), 71
Clark, J.P., 67, 136, 141, 142
code-switching, 96-101, 107, 108, 110, 139, 142, 143, 145
Collins English Dictionary, 91
Columbus, 62
Communication Skills Project (COMSKIP), 57
COMSKIPTECH, 57
Conrad, Joseph, 123
Corona Schools, 41, 43, 44
creoles, 3, 4, 5, 6, 32, 62, 63, 65, 151; Cameroon, 4; Gullah, 4; Guyana, 4: Jamaican, 6; Saramaccan, 4; Sierra Leone, 9; Surinam, 4; West Indies, 9
Cross River State, 27
Crowther, Samuel Ajayi, first African bishop, 13, 16
Crumwell, Alex, 13, 123
Cugoano,, Ottobah, 11, 122
Cummings, E.E., 132, 133

Dalzel, Archibald, 2
Death and the King's horseman (Soyinka) 130
Denmark, 147
diatopic variety, 73, 74, 83
diatypic variety, 73, 83, 91, 97, 99, 100
Dictionary of West African English, 94 n 8
Duke, Antera, 11, 70

Earth (a poem) (Osundare), 137-138
Efik, 35, 127
Elizabeth my lover (Olisa), 139-140
endonormative, 80, 82, 92, 120 n 6, 148
England, church of, 71
'English, broken,' 2, 9, 75
English, broken,' 2, 9, 75
English for special purposes (ESP), 151-152
English language, creative uses of, 69-71; official record-keeping of, 67-69; tenors in the, 23-24
Equiano, Olaudah, 11, 13, 122-123; *Interesting narrative of the life of ... or Gustavus Vassa the African,* 123
exonormative, 80, 82, 92, 148

Feather woman of the jungle (Tutuola), 133-134
Fodio, Uthman dan, 21
Ford Foundation (USA), 57
Fourah Bay College, Freetown, 20
France, 62, 64, 114
Ghana, 13,, 66

Index

Grieve report (1964), 47 59 n 11
Guinea Coast, 2
Gustavus Vassa the African (Equiano), 123

Hansard, 68
Hausa (language), 22-28, 33, 41, 68, 69, 75, 76, 81, 97, 102, 110, 149
Hong Kong, 62
Hope Waddel Institute, Calabar, 1, 15, 45
Huxley, Elspeth, 121, 1326

Ibadan, University College, (1948), 43, 44; University of, 52, 57; Arts Theatre, 141; Department of Communication and Language Arts, 60 n 112; Department of Language Arts, 53, 60n12; International School of 44; Reading Centre, 52-53, Staff School of, 43
Idanre (a poem) (Soyinka), 136
Ifa gnomic poetry, 136
Ife, University of, 112
Ife Six Year Primary Project, 43, 50, 57,, 59 n 9
Igbo, 97, 123, 128; language, 22, 26, 27, 28, 33, 68, 75, 76, 81, 97, 109-110, 129, 130, 142, 149
Igbobi College, Lagos, founded in 1932, 46
India, 36, 62, 65, 66, 67, 148
Interesting narrative of the life of... or Gustavus Vassa the African (Equiano). 123
Interpreters, The (Soyinka), 129
King's College, Lagos, 45
Krio, 4; Sierra Leone, 3, 6, 32
Kwa language, 24, 76
Lagos, 44
language - mixing, 100-112, 116, 143, 145
Language Teacher, 58
lexical borrowing, 101, 110, 115
lingua franca, 23, 24, 26-28, 34, 63, 67, 69, 81, 124, 147, 148, 149, 154
Lion and the jewel, The (Soyinka), 130
Liverpool, 2

London, 64; University of, 43, 52
Lugard, Lord, 1, 58 n 1

Madmen and specialists (Soyinka), 130
Masquerade, 142, 143, 144
Methodist Boys' High School, Lagos, 45
mother tongue, 64, 65, 69, 70, 72, 73, 79, 81, 93, 95, 96, 98, 99, 100, 115, 123, 132, 133, 134, 147, 149, 150, 153, 154

national language, objective criteria for the choice of, 29-34
National Policy on Language in Education, 149, 150, 154
National Universities Commission (NUC), 55
'new Englishes', 63-64, 67, 125
New Zealand, 29, 62, 67, 147
Nigeria, amalgamation of Northern and Southern Protectorates, 1, 58 n 1; characteristics of the Use of English in, 72-93; commerce in, 1-11; creation of Mid-West Region (1963), 27; cultural history of, 123; education in, 14-20; educational activities of missionaries in, 15-17, 20, 21; Federal Ministry of Education, National Language Centre, 57-58; missionary activity in, 11, 12, 14;
Nigeria (contd), policies on development of English in, 20-34; primary schools in, 35-45; religion in, 11-14; secondary schools in, 45-52; unity schools, 26; the university in, 52-58
Nigerian biligualism, features of, 96 - 1..,.
Nigerian Educational Research and Development Centre, merged with National Language Centre, 58
Nigerian English, 92-93, 96, 141, 150, 151
No longer at ease (Achebe), 127-128
Norway, 147
Nsukka, University of Nigeria, 53, 57

Okara, Gabriel, 132; *The Voice*, 135

Okigbo, 129
Olisa, Okwenwa, *Elizabeth my lover*, 140
Onitsha market literature, 143, 144
Onitsha popular literature, 136, 139-140
Osofisan, Femi, 139
Osoogun, 13
Osundare, Niyi, *Earth* (a poem), 138-139
Oxford English Dictionary, 114

Palmwine drinkard (Tutuola), 67, 121
pidgin, 31, 32, 63, 65, 69, 70, 75, 99, 100, 124, 129, 139, 140, 141, 142, 143; 145; English, 5; minimal, 2, 8, 9, 14; Nigerian, 2, 3, 5-11, 27, 31-32; origin of, 8, Portuguese, 3, 5.
Polyglotta Africana, 14
Portugal, 29

Queen's College, Lagos, 45

Reading, University of (England), 57
Rivers State, 27
Rockefeller Foundation (USA), 52
Rome, Church of, 71
Rotimi, Ola, 139

St. Andrew's College, Oyo, 1, 45
Sancho, Ignatius, 11, 122
Scottish Presbyterian Church (Calabar), 15
Shakespeare, William, 139
Sierra Leone, 11, 14, 19, 21; English education in, 13
Singapore; 64
slave trade, 11; abolition of, 12
Soyinka, Wole, 67, 125, 126, 128, 129, 133, 139, 141, 142; *Animistic spells*, 137; *Death and the King's horseman*, 130; *Idanre* (a poem), 137; *The Interpreters*, 130; *The Lion and the jewel*, 130; *Madmen and specialists*, 130
Spain, 29

standard Nigerian English, 85, 86, 89-93, 139, 153
Straight for English (a course book), 41
Sranam, 3, 4
Surinam, 3, 4
Sweden, 148
Switzerland, 34

Things fall apart (Achebe), 147 n 8
Thomas, Dylan, 121, 133
Tutuola, Amos, 132, 133, 135; *Feather woman of the jungle*, 134-135; *Palmwine drinkard*, 67, 121
Twain, Mark, 133

United Nations, 64
United States of America (USA), 19, 29, 62, 67, 82, 148

Village Headmaster, the, 139, 143, 145
Voice, the (Okara), 135
Wesley College, Ibadan, 45
West Africa English, 92
West African Examinations Council, 18, 54, 91; Oral English of the, 48, 49, 50; International Panel on the English Language of the, 48; Tests Development and Research Office (TEDRO) of the, 48, 49, 50
West Indies, 62
Wheatley, Phillis, 122
Wooden gong, the (Akpan), 127

Yoruba, 6, 7, 27, 97, 98, 132, 133, 134, 137, 139; *language*, 22, 26, 28, 33, 68, 69, 75, 76, 81, 97, 98, 99, 102, 104-106, 107-112, 115-119, 130, 151; *mythology*; 137; *Ogun myth*, 134.

Zambia, 65

www.ingramcontent.com/pod-product-compliance
Lightning Source LLC
Chambersburg PA
CBHW051526230426
43668CB00012B/1754